Ordinary People, Extraordinary God

SERMONS FOR SUNDAYS
AFTER PENTECOST
FIRST HALF

Ordinary People, Extraordinary God

SERMONS FOR SUNDAYS
AFTER PENTECOST
FIRST HALF

CYCLE B
FIRST LESSON TEXTS

ROBERT A. NOBLETT

C.S.S. Publishing Co., Inc.
Lima, Ohio

ORDINARY PEOPLE, EXTRAORDINARY GOD

Copyright © 1990 by
The C.S.S. Publishing Company, Inc.
Lima, Ohio

All rights reserved. No part of this publication may be reproduced, stored in a retrieval system, or transmitted in any form or by any means, electronic, mechanical, photocopying, recording, or otherwise, without the prior permission of the publisher. Inquiries should be addressed to: The C.S.S. Publishing Company, Inc., 628 South Main Street, Lima, Ohio 45804.

Library of Congress in Publication Data
Noblett, Robert A., 1943-
   Ordinary people, extraordinary God : sermons for Sundays after Pentecost / Robert A. Noblett.
     p.   cm.
   ISBN 1-55673-259-7
   1. Bible. O.T. — Sermons. 2. Sermons, American. 3. Baptists-Sermons. I. Title.
BX6333.N48607   1991
252'.6—dc20   90-35083
                                                                                       CIP

9037 / ISBN 1-55673-259-7   PRINTED IN U.S.A.

To our parents:

*Robert Maxwell Earl
Archie Borden Noblett
May Elizabeth Noblett*

In memory of:

Josephine Bair Earl

Contents

Preface

Holy Trinity	*Isaiah 6:1-8*	**God's Flowing and our Ebbing**	11
Proper 4	*1 Samuel 16:1-13*	**In Search of a Leader**	19
Proper 5	*1 Samuel 16:14-23*	**Music As Prescription**	27
Proper 6	*2 Samuel 1:1, 17-27*	**A Song Sung Blue**	33
Proper 7	*2 Samuel 5:1-12*	**Leading As Loving**	39
Proper 8	*2 Samuel 6:1-15*	**An Untouchable God?**	47
Proper 9	*2 Samuel 7:1-17*	**A Sleeping Bag God**	55
Proper 10	*2 Samuel 7:18-29*	**A Thanksgiving Checklist**	63
Proper 11	*2 Samuel 11:1-15*	**David and the Devil**	69
Proper 12	*2 Samuel 12:1-14*	**Speaking Truth to Power**	75
Proper 13	*2 Samuel 12:15b-24*	**When Matters Hang in the Balance**	81
Proper 14	*2 Samuel 18:1, 5, 9-15*	**Runaway Lives**	87
Proper 15	*2 Samuel 18:24-33*	**From Mourning to Morning**	93
Proper 16	*2 Samuel 23:1-7*	**Swansong as Themesong**	99

Preface

These lectionary-based sermons have to do with themes that run through all our lives: grief, music, gratitude, fear, evil, uncertainty, leadership, faith and more. In a sense they are far ranging, and yet within any twenty-four-hour period, many of these themes will move in and out of our consciousness. They represent the life-stuff of ordinary people like you and me. But more to the point, they — potentially at least — are places in our lives where our ordinariness can be the focus of God's extraordinary grace. Hence the title, *Ordinary People, Extraordinary God.*

The sermons were originally preached in the congregation I presently serve, the First Baptist Church of Carbondale, Illinois (American Baptist), and were then slightly edited for publication. I salute my congregation for their encouragement and loving support.

My appreciation goes out also to my wife Ruth for her unswerving encouragement in this task, and for her careful reading of the manuscript and attentiveness to technical matters.

The preaching ministry is simultaneously a wonderful and taxing opportunity to be vessels of God's grace. We accept it mindful that God's word to Paul is God's word to us, too: "My grace is sufficient for you, for my power is made perfect in weakness." (2 Corinthians 12:9)

Robert Noblett
Carbondale, Illinois

God's Flowing and Our Ebbing

The Holy Trinity   *Isaiah 6:1-8*

My family and I have spent several enjoyable vacations on the Atlantic Ocean, both at Cape Cod and along the rock-bound coast of Maine. Always we have enjoyed the beaches and the pastimes attendant to them. One perennial pastime is the building of sand castles, and I well remember our children building them close to the sea's edge and how, with tidal changes, the parameters of the ebbing and flowing would be altered, often allowing the ocean to become increasingly bold in assailing what the children had so carefully created.

There are corresponding patterns in human life. It could be said that in sleeping we ebb and upon rising, flow. Or in conversation between two persons, one becomes quiet (ebbs) so that the other can talk (flow).

This celebrated sixth chapter of Isaiah is likewise about ebbing and flowing. At the outset, it is about God flowing and Isaiah ebbing; then later, it is about Isaiah flowing again — as he never had before.

The powerful phrasing of this account offers insight relative to the central issue in this religious encounter.

Ordinary People, Extraordinary God

High and Lifted Up

In the year that King Uzziah died I saw the Lord sitting upon a throne, high and lifted up . . .

(Isaiah 6:1)

That's God flowing.

"I saw the Lord . . ." Often, very often, we see much less.

Occasionally, someone will give us a photographic representation of one thing or another, designed in such a way that initially we may have a difficult time discerning anything but shadings and blobs of light and darkness. But if we are persistent, and perhaps turn the photograph around and look at it from different perspectives, eventually we spot what has been there all along. Until that time, however, we find ourselves distracted by seemingly meaningless configurations.

This happens religiously, too. In fact, with great regularity the church becomes sidetracked by what is peripheral and inconsequential, and dupes itself right out of that fundamental encounter that is the prime motivating factor of all that we do in the church.

Worship is a good case in point. For worship to be all it can be for people, there are certain ancillary factors which, when they are firmly in place, can be most helpful. Good ushering, comfortable temperatures, readable orders of worship, organ and choral responses — these are all wonderful aids to worship.

But often we get sidetracked by such issues. We center on what ultimately doesn't matter and fail to be transported into the presence of God.

Just as the windows on our automobiles need not be squeaky-clean in order for us to have the necessary visibility to drive, so worship does not need to be an impeccable production in order for us to see God. When it is with all our

Pentecost I

hearts that we truly seek him, God will come — even if every jot and tittle is not in place.

This is to say that in worship there needs to be a straining and a stretching beyond the liturgical movements; because in so doing, we begin to posture ourselves to be grasped by the spirit of the living God. It is not, mind you, the God we have created through the juxtaposing of liturgical designs, but the God who is always there waiting to meet his people.

And Isaiah reminds us that God will not be domesticated by us. There is an "*awe*fulness" and an unfathomable mystery about God. The observation of Phillips Brooks, offered a century ago, still stands:

> *We talk about God's incomprehensibleness as if it were a sad necessity; as if, if we could understand God through and through, it would be happier and better for us. The intimation of Isaiah's vision is something different from that. It is the glory of his seraphim that they stand in the presence of a God so great that they can never comprehend Him. His brightness overwhelms them; they cover their faces with their wings, and their hearts are filled with reverence, which is the first of the conditions of complete human life which they represent . . . No man does anything well who does not feel the unknown surrounding and pressing upon the known, and who is not therefore aware all the time that what he does has deeper sources and more distant issues than he can comprehend. (Phillips Brooks,* Selected Sermons, *p. 84)*

"I saw the Lord . . ." Beyond all else, that's what people should declare when they leave the sanctuary.

Woe Is Me

> *And I said: "Woe is me! For I am lost; for I am a man of unclean lips, and I dwell in the midst of a people of unclean lips; for my eyes have seen the King, the Lord of hosts!"*
>
> (Isaiah 6:5)

Ordinary People, Extraordinary God

That's Isaiah ebbing.

In the original Broadway version of *Carousel* there was a song that for some reason never made it into the film version. The main character, a barker who has led a less than savory life, asks in a fist-shaking manner, "Take me before the highest throne and let me be judged by the highest judge of all." There is a sense of defiance in his voice and this is the very antithesis of what we see here in the religious experience of Isaiah. Far more typical is Job saying, ". . . I despise myself, and repent in dust and ashes" (Job 42:6) or Jeremiah declaring, "My heart is broken within me, all my bones shake; I am like a drunken man, like a man overcome by wine, because of the Lord and because of his holy words." (Jeremiah 23:9) When people have a sense for the splendor and majesty of God, it leads them not to flex their muscles, but to bow their knees.

Please understand that what Isaiah confesses does not fly in the face of our efforts to make people feel fundamentally good about themselves. "Woe is me" is not about undermining self-esteem and making people go around feeling terrible about themselves. Instead it has to do with feelings that inevitably follow when we find our very real humanity — warts and all — juxtaposed to the holiness of God. It is to existentially understand the rhetorical question of the psalmist, "If thou, O Lord, shouldst mark iniquities, Lord, who could stand?" (Psalm 130:3)

Imagine, for a moment, that you are a twelve-year-old elementary school student and you are just learning to play the violin. If you have ever attended an elementary school orchestra concert, you will remember the variant sounds produced by the neophyte. Your first orchestra concert is recorded, and when you get home it is played back for you on the family stereo system. Then imagine immediately thereafter listening to a recording of Beethoven's *Concerto For Violin and Orchestra in D Major* played by violin virtuoso Isaac

Pentecost I

Stern. You would quickly develop an awareness for the difference between fledgling emergence and seasoned perfection. The difference would be overwhelmingly striking.

Isaiah is describing the immense difference between our humanity and God's holiness. Moments of that nature remind us that we are creaturely and derived. Far from mocking us, they recall for us whose we are.

Your Guilt Is Taken Away

But in this difference we are not left to falter and grovel.

And he touched my mouth, and said: "Behold, this has touched your lips; your guilt is taken away, and your sin is forgiven."

(Isaiah 6:7)

One of the attending creatures Isaiah saw in his vision takes a firestone from the incense altar of the temple, touches Isaiah's lips and removes his guilt. We allegedly modern types don't always know what to make of seraphims, burning coals and the like, but the crucial point is that Isaiah is touched by God through this attending creature, and experiences forgiveness. This firestone becomes, as it were, the kiss of God, and Isaiah is redeemed.

If we could in some way weigh the guilt brought into each of our sanctuaries sabbath by sabbath, how heavy would it all be, do you think? A few pounds? Twenty-pounds? A staggering number of pounds? I tend to think in terms of the latter. It would be significant poundage. Most of us come to the present shackled with more than our share of guilt for what has or has not happened in the past. It can be guilt about what we have done or failed to do, about feelings we have had (and perhaps still do) but feel we shouldn't. Maybe it is guilt about thoughts we have had.

Ordinary People, Extraordinary God

The good news from Isaiah is that God is waiting to send a seraphim in our direction, carrying a burning coal, to burn our guilt away. And, just maybe, the difficulty we have in feeling grace and forgiveness has more to do with our unwillingness to accept them than with God not bestowing them. Thomas John Carlisle is insightful:

*It is not enough
to be forgiven —
though God is prompt.*

*It may take longer
to accept the fact
we are forgiven.*

*And even longer
to become inclined
to share forgiveness.*

(*Alive Now!* May/June 1981, p. 42)

Has the seraphim of God drawn near to you and me, carrying the burning coal of forgiveness, only to find our hands defensively outstretched, desirous of keeping that distance from God that insures our continuing misery? Are we ebbing when God would have us flow?

Send Me

Hence the resolution of it all for Isaiah:

And I heard the voice of the Lord saying, "Whom shall I send, and who will go for us?" Then I said, "Here am I! Send me."

(Isaiah 6:8)

Pentecost I

What an amazing sequence of events! Brought into the blazing and incomprehensible presence of God, painfully aware of his finitude and transitoriness in the presence of the Eternal, forgiven and now commissioned — invited to flow.

God, Isaiah's commissioning reminds us, is not looking for superstars and flawless people (even if they were available!). God is perfectly able to take our brokenness, our faith and lack of faith, our energy and lack of energy, and use us for kingdom purposes.

Nothing new, this. It is nothing short of the bedrock rhythm of the Christian faith. We celebrate it every time we worship, even if we don't fully understand or comprehend it. God can take very ordinary, unsung and fallen people like you and me and utilize our lives as the vessels of his grace.

The psalmist very neatly ties together what this commissioning of Isaiah declares: "... a broken and contrite heart, O God, thou wilt not despise." (Psalm 51:17)

At the point of our deepest ebbing, God turns the tide, reclaims us, and invites us to flow toward and for the Kingdom.

In Search of a Leader

Proper 4   *1 Samuel 16:1-13*

Anyone who has served on a nominating committee knows how crucial talented leadership is to any group, including the body of Christ. God, our story reminds us, shares that concern. God is unhappy with Saul's leadership and sends Samuel on a mission to secure a replacement.

Look Who Is Doing the Calling

Perhaps the most salient features of this story is the fact that it is God who is doing the calling, with Samuel as his agent. Leaders in the church vary in their understanding of the call to ministry, but all would agree that in church vocations (vocation comes from a Latin derivative meaning "to call") there needs to be some sense of being summoned to a particular ministry and summoned to that ministry by God. It is that underlying sense of having been summoned that makes Christian leadership distinctive from securing a job simply in order to have something to do or to pay the bills.

Ordinary People, Extraordinary God

Clearly, there are occasions when the sense of call has been too casual or easy or even bizarre a matter, as it was, so the story goes, for a man who had been a farmer. One hot humid day, while escaping the weather's oppressiveness by sitting under the shade-bestowing branches of a tree, the farmer looked up and saw a cloud formation that looked precisely like the letters "g" and "p." Seeing that, the man knew in an instant that he had been called to the ministry, for surely those letters were God's way of saying to him, "Go preach." A friend, with whom the farmer was sharing this experience, asked him, "Did you ever consider the possibility that God was telling you, 'Go plow'?"

Struggling with a call to ministry lends validity and depth to any ministry that follows in its wake; and even if the struggle ends in the sense that there has not been a call, that struggling, at the very least, lends integrity to one's life. To deal with questions of origin and destination, of sustenance and truth, is no mean matter and it should be no cause for wonderment that the author of Hebrews declares, "It is a fearful thing to fall into the hands of the living God." (Hebrews 10:31)

A few years back Beverly Gaventa addressed the graduating classes of Colgate Rochester Divinity School, Bexley Hall, and Crozer Theological Seminary, and on that occasion raised the issue of the distinctive nature of vocation. She commented:

> *I raise this issue tonight because I think that we have lost a proper understanding of vocation. We have domesticated the term; it has become a stage in the bureaucracy of ordination. Individuals are asked whether they have a "calling" and are expected to respond with a one word answer. My fear is that we have lost not only a "doctrine" of vocation, but a sense of vocation as well.*

Professor Gaventa shared Paul Minear's description of vocation:

Pentecost I

> *The sense of vocation . . . gives a person a point of origin around which his memories can coalesce, a destination that can include all expectations, and a set of priorities that enables him to order his conflicting desires . . . [Vocation] connotes an identity conferred on a person and accepted by that person as his own.*
> (*Bulletin From the Hill*, June 1982, p. 3)

One cannot speak of Christian vocations without immediately implying the role of God in that process, and arduously struggling with that dimension bestows upon one's life (and one's ministry too if one feels that God is indeed doing the calling), a blessed sense of redemptive struggle.

Not As We Judge

In God's search for a leader, our story also reminds us that in matters of evaluation, God's criteria are apt to be different from ours.

The man I am remembering was quite polished. He found it easy to speak in front of groups; he was able to pray spontaneously whenever asked; he was supportive of church programs; he would often show up at people's homes at the point of crisis; he had a kind of avuncular way about him. People in the church family would regularly comment, "Harry should have been a minister."

If this person had ever appeared on that old television show where three persons presented themselves as having a particular identity and then folks in the audience voted for the one who was authentic, more than a few would have pointed to Harry and aped Samuel's words when he beheld Jesse's son Eliab: "This man standing here in the Lord's presence is surely the one he has chosen." (1 Samuel 16:6 TEV)

Ordinary People, Extraordinary God

But all the protestations never took root within me. Harry, as I experienced him, fulfilled Thomas Merton's description of what he called "the plaster saint":

> *The stereotyped image is easy to sketch out here: it is essentially an image without the slightest moral flaw. . . . He flings himself into fire, ice water or briers rather than even face a remote occasion of sin. His intentions are always the noblest. His words are always the most edifying cliches, fitting the situation with a devastating obviousness that silences even the thought of dialogue. Indeed, the "perfect" in this fearsome sense are elevated above the necessity or even the capacity for a fully human dialogue with their fellow men. They are without humor as they are without wonder, without feeling and without interest in the common affairs of mankind. Yet of course they always rush to the scene with the precise act of virtue called for by every situation. They are always there kissing the leper's sores at the very moment when the king and his noble attendants come around the corner and stop in their tracks, mute in admiration . . .*
>
> (*Life and Holiness*, pp. 18-19)

We do not need ministers, ordained or lay, like that. They retard the beauty of an incarnational faith, God expressing himself through the humanness of life. Disciples who are themselves, warts and all, are infinitely more winsome than those who try to pass themselves off as the very embodiment of holiness and succeed only in establishing that they are its very antithesis. God is not looking for blow-dried, glib-tongued, unctuous sons and daughters; God is calling authentic sons and daughters who see in themselves what Paul saw in himself: "So I find it to be a law that when I want to do right, evil lies close to hand." (Romans 7:21)

"But the Lord said to him, 'Pay no attention to how tall and handsome he is. I have rejected him, because I do not

Pentecost I

judge as man judges. Man looks at the outward appearance, but I look at the heart.' " (1 Samuel 16:7 TEV)

There Is Still the Youngest

After eight interviews Samuel is still batting zero. "Do you have more sons?" Samuel asks Jesse. Yes, Jesse does, but he seemed such an unlikely candidate that he wasn't even thought to be in the running. "There is still the youngest, but he is out taking care of the sheep." (1 Samuel 16:11 TEV) The call goes out to this youngest son and the Lord says to Samuel. "This is the one — anoint him." (1 Samuel 16:12 TEV)

God, it seems, is a God of surprises. We look for God in the west and God comes from the east; we search in vain for God in the south, and God comes from the north. We want God now, but are told that those who wait for God shall find their strength renewed. We conceive of God in categories of strength, but find God in vulnerability. We think to dress God in robes regal and resplendent, and behold, God comes as a baby. We think God's choice will be one thing, and much to our chagrin, it is quite another. The Gospel is full of surprises and reversals, and God, as the psalmist expresses it, has often "given us wine that makes us stagger" in astonishment. (Psalm 60:4 NEB)

That God should surprise us in the area of Christian leadership should then be no cause for surprise. It has always been that way. ". . . God chose what is foolish in the world," says Paul, "to shame the wise, God chose what is weak in the world to shame the strong, God chose what is low and despised in the world, even things that are not, to bring to nothing things that are. . . ." (1 Corinthians 1:27-28) That is still the pattern of God. Regularly God's presence flows from lives we would never take, at first glance or even fifth glance, to be potential channels of grace.

Ordinary People, Extraordinary God

An Accompanying Spirit

The story ends, "Immediately the spirit of the Lord took control of David and was with him from that day on." (1 Samuel 16:13 TEV)

". . . and was with him from that day on." That truth alludes us. It is easy to fall into the trap where we pay too handsomely for the salutes of those around us and forget that our strength is ultimately in the presence of God. If we don't have that awareness going for us, then Christian leaders quickly become sychophants who pour syrup on anyone's waffles for a pat on the back, deserved or not.

When I was installed as minister of the First Baptist Church of Milton, Massachuetts, many years ago, a friend, Mahlon Gilbert, gave me a card and I have kept it. It has three panels. The first panel pictures a missile-like object speeding down from on high and heading directly toward a snail on the ground below. The missile is many times the size of the snail. The second panel shows the missile squarely and forcefully hitting the snail. In the third panel the snail is wholly intact, but the missile lays broken in two, next to the snail. The two halves of the missile appear to be looking at each other and in amazement asking, "What on earth has happened?!" Mahlon's note to me that day said:

> Bob:
>
> *There is nothing more one needs in the ministry with a congregation than an understanding of the theological and personal truths of this card.*
> *Blessings upon your work in Milton.*

For a time as I thought about that card, I identified the minister with the missile and thought this to be the message: Don't come down too hard on your congregation or they will break you in two! For some, perhaps, that would be an accurate reading.

Pentecost I

But later I came to identify the minister with the snail and the missile with what sometimes does happen to the minister, or other Christian leaders for that matter, in a congregation. Whenever we don the mantle of leadership, missiles will occasionally come our way. Of that we can be sure. But they need not become our undoing. For beyond what men and women can give us, as precious as all that can at times no doubt be, our ultimate strength is rooted in the Lord of hosts.

God is always involved in the search for leaders. God is searching hearts right this moment and looks not for perfection, but for faithfulness. And when the missiles come, if God has truly called us, our leadership will be nourished by that "peace of God, which passes all understanding." (Philippians 4:7)

Music as Prescription

Proper 5   *1 Samuel 16:14-23*

Let's suppose you have been feeling distressed and fatigued of late and this has manifested itself in some physical symptoms. You've been having headaches; your lower back has been aching; and there has been a great deal of tightness around your neck and shoulders. Off to your family physician you trek, and after she has examined you, this is what she says: "You are suffering from unmitigated stress and I prescribe the following. Each morning when you arise and each evening before bedtime, listen for one half hour to music and choose from one of the following: Debussy's *Afternoon of a Fawn*, Bach's *Jesu, Joy of Man's Desiring*, Samuel Barber's *Adagio For Strings*, or Aaron Copeland's *Appalachian Spring*."

Sound surprising? It would be, because we are just at the starting line in understanding and utilizing the therapeutic nature of music. Sound novel? It shouldn't, because the servants of Saul in the latter days of the monarchy knew the power of music to heal and prescribed it for their king.

Ordinary People, Extraordinary God

> Let our lord now command your servants, who are before you, to seek out a man who is skillful in playing the lyre; and when the evil spirit from God is upon you, he will play it, and you will be well.
>
> (1 Samuel 16:16)

David is the musician of choice and he proves himself to be effective in that role.

> ... whenever the evil spirit from God was upon Saul, David took the lyre and played it with his hand; so Saul was refreshed, and was well, and the evil spirit departed from him.
>
> (1 Samuel 16:23)

A Powerful Medium

What are we to make of this story? Clearly it presents music as a powerful medium. It has undeniable potency.

Avram Goldstein of Standford University has studied what gives people thrills. In examining the self-reports of more than 250 people, Avram found that at the bottom of the list was the parade. But ninety-six percent of the respondents indicated receiving a thrill from a musical passage. In fact, a musical passage was at the top of the list, even beating out by over twenty percentage points sexual activity. (*Psychology Today*, December 1985, p. 50)

It is therefore little cause for wonderment that music commands so much of our energy, time and money. Never are we far from it. Most of the time, it is a twist of the knob or a push of the button away. We listen to it, react to it, revel in it, sing it, and some of us write it.

Clearly, music has a special place in the life of the church. Its importance to the church is manifested in a variety of ways

Pentecost I

and is even acknowledged in a backhanded way by the fact that musical matters sometimes occasion spirited debate and even outright conflict within church families. One can also see the value imputed to music in the efforts of denominational families to publish new hymnals, update old ones, and encourage the writing of new hymns.

A Focused Power

But more than simply being a powerful medium, music demonstrates intent. It is a resource with many purposes. It can beam its sounds on many human problems and can open the heart to many joys.

Anne Rosenfeld has called music "the beautiful disturber" and comments, "Music can move us to tears or to dance, to fight or make love. It can inspire our most exalted religious feelings and ease our anxious and lonely moments. Its pleasures are many, but it can also be alien, irksome, almost maddening." (*Psychology Today*, December 1985, p. 48)

Some music summons us to action. "Rise up, O Men of God" is a hymn of that genre, and often marches and overtures do that, too.

Music can also be a form of protest. The folk songs of the sixties and seventies were that and in 1916 Carl Nielsen, the Danish composer, wrote his *Symphony No. 4* which was understood to be a protest against the First World War and an affirmation of human worth. It was called *The Inextinguishable*.

Often music soothes and restores. First Samuel is not clear about the nature of that "evil spirit" that regularly afflicted King Saul, but there is a strong implication that it was agitation of one kind or another, and the music created by David on the lyre made him feel refreshed and well again. "It is my observation," writes Donald Houts, "that while the arts have generally been appreciated at an intellectual level, they have not been fully exploited for their therapeutic, restorative, and reconciling capacities." (*The Journal of Pastoral Care*, September, 1981)

Inspiration is another function of music. It can restore our vision and lift us to a greater level of appreciation and motivation.

A Channel of God's Grace

Best of all, music is a channel for the grace of God. God's presence is always a meditated one, and like the burning bush, music is yet another vessel of service in God's disclosure to his people.

Robert McAfee Brown has said this about the close association between theology and music:

> *There has always been a close association between theology and music . . . No theological statement of divine ineffability can begin to compare with the wonder of mystery communicated by Beethoven's last string quartets, particularly the Cavatina in Opus 130 and the opening fugue in Opus 131. If we wish to enter into the spirit of medieval faith, we had better not only read St. Thomas' 24-volume Summa but also listen to (or, better yet, sing ourselves) St. Francis' "Canticle of the Sun."*
>
> (*Theology in a New Key*)

Many years ago a friend who is a musician introduced me to Frederick Chopin's *C Minor Prelude*. I would contend that one cannot hear this piece and the words written for it and not feel enwrapped in the presence of the risen Christ. The music becomes the vehicle through which the hope and

Pentecost I

affirmation of the words come to live in the life of the person hearing them. They are basically simple words:

Christ be with me.
Christ within me.
Christ beside me.
Christ, too, in me.
Christ to comfort and restore me.
Christ behind me.
Christ before me.

Christ in quiet.
Christ in danger.
Christ in mouth of friend or stranger.
Christ in hearts of all that love me.
Christ beneath me.
Christ above me.

We look for healing in medical therapies, relaxation techniques, journal writing, prayer, talking, diet and untold other places. We need also to rediscover what happened to King Saul when David picked up the lyre. ". . . David took the lyre and played it . . . Saul was refreshed . . . and was well . . . and the evil spirit departed from him." (1 Samuel 16:23)

A Song Sung Blue

Proper 6   *2 Samuel 1:1, 17-27*

Years ago, Neil Diamond wrote and recorded a song that became quite popular; it was entitled "Song Sung Blue." The lyrics have long left me, but that title came rushing back when I began looking at David's lament for Saul and Jonathan. That's a good definition of a lament — a song sung blue.

A Medium for Grief

At first this might strike us as a bit strange — singing our grief — but there it clearly is in the first chapter of 2 Samuel:

> *Ye daughters of Israel, weep over*
>   *Saul,*
> *who clothed you daintily in scarlet,*
> *who put ornaments of gold upon*
>   *your apparel.*

Ordinary People, Extraordinary God

> *How are the mighty fallen
> in the midst of the battle!*
>
> *Jonathan lies slain upon thy high
> places.
> I am distressed for you, my brother
> Jonathan;
> very pleasant have you been to me;
> your love to me was wonderful,
> passing the love of women.*
>
> (2 Samuel 1:24-26)

Actually, singing about grief isn't that unusual at all. If we are attentive to the titles and lyrics of the songs that flood the airwaves about us, we discover that all the time people are singing laments over their disappointments and discouragements and failures. We need only call to mind the genre of music called "the blues" or the lyrics of some country and western songs and we hear about broken hearts, homes, and hopes. Rock music, likewise, expresses those concerns. A recent listing of rock songs that young people most enjoy included these titles:

"Roll With It"
"I Don't Want to Live Without Your Love"
"Please Don't Go Girl"
"I Don't Wanna Go On With You Like That"
"I Hate Myself For Loving You"
"Fallen Angel"

What David is doing is done all the time.

Laments over Laments

It's done all the time, but one easily gets the impression that even in the Christian community — a community that continually hears the psalms, knows about Jesus' teachings on grief and knows full well that crucifixion preceded resurrection — there is sometimes subtly related the not-so-subtle suggestion that Christians should always be joyful and that if they must be sad, they should be sad in private. Tears of disappointment and grief, expressions of sadness born of failure and tragedy — these are best shed in the privacy of one's home after everyone else has gone to bed. Cry there, if you want to and must, but certainly not on the sabbath when everyone else has risen to sing a rousing rendition of "Joyful, Joyful," or not in the church school class when the teacher has spent considerable time preparing and certainly wouldn't want you to pour your tears all over his stellar lesson on the first chapter of Second Thessalonians.

Pardon me, if that's in order, but I choose to differ with this ill-founded contention. I differ if we are talking about bona fide grief and disappointment, legitimate lamenting if you will, and not about chronic complaining and a regularly fed appetite for a discontented spirit. They are not the same thing. Grief is something through which we must pass; with chronic complaining we have taken up a residence.

We hear a great deal in our day about positive Christianity, but please understand that Christianity that is authentically positive incorporates into itself the inevitability and rightfulness of sometimes feeling disappointed and saddened.

Grief as Witness

It occurs to me, moreover, that the measure of our grief can easily be the measure of the meaning we have derived from a relationship, or an assignment, or an experience. It can be understood to be a barometer of our investment; when that investment has been significant and we are asked to divest, it brings pain. There is no way around that.

Ordinary People, Extraordinary God

I heard a beautiful lament (not a complaint, mind you, but a lament) a short time ago. It was from a beautiful, ninety-five plus, legally blind, now crippled, but always engaging Christian woman named Elsie. Her waking moments are now totally spent in a recliner. A while back she was told she needed an operation if her life was to be prolonged for a time, and she elected to go for the additional time. She spoke of this in her characteristically delightful way: "It was," Elsie said, "like being asked whether I wanted to be hung or shot."

When Elsie talks, her words are interspersed with high-pitched sounds, a whining of sorts, but not the kind of whining we associate with agitation or chronic complaining. Rather, it is a whining expressive of her sense for life's fullness and God's goodness. It is more like the singing of whales, clearly a language, but not a language imprisoned in the twenty-six letters of an alphabet.

Elsie laments what has happened and is happening to her, but it is lamenting that is dynamic and not static. Her whining is a way through which Elsie is pushing the limits of her life up against the reality of death so that she can win through to death's beyond.

So it is that we have this sad song from David, so thoroughly soaked with the importance and richness of his friendship with both Saul and Saul's son Jonathan. It is as though a tiny video camera has been inserted into David's soul and there on the television screen before us is some of what has filled that soul with meaning and purpose.

Grief as a measure of value is, I believe, what Henri Nouwen is describing in a passage from *A Letter of Consolation*. He is writing to his father about the death of the woman who was for the one mother, and the other wife:

> *If time does anything, it deepens our grief. The longer we live, the more fully we become aware of who she was for us, and the more intimately we experience what her love*

meant to us. Real, deep love is, as you know, very unobtrusive, seemingly easy and obvious, and so present that we take it for granted. Therefore, it is often only in retrospect — or better, in memory — that we fully realize its power and depth. Yes, indeed, love often makes itself visible in pain. The pain we are now experiencing shows us how deep, full, intimate, and all-pervasive her love was.
(pp. 16-17)

Toward Resolution

Finally, a song sung blue implies that there is movement from one point to another. There is a struggling, a reckoning, an effect to understand, integrate and resolve. Whether or not we literally sing, this musical imagery captures the essential dynamism that must be there if resolution is to occur. Remember Tevye in *Fiddler on the Roof* lamenting his economic state? "If I Were a Rich Man" is the lament he sings and one gains the impression, hearing Tevye sing, that the lamenting is therapeutic and affords him some sense, if not of resolution, at least of relief.

Frederick Buechner has put it this way:

Listen to your life. See it for the fathomless mystery that it is. In the boredom and pain of it no less than in the excitement and gladness: touch, taste, smell your way to the holy and hidden heart of it because in the last analysis all moments are key moments, and life itself is grace.
(Now and Then, p. 87)

There is a time to lament, as David lamented, and during those moments we have this assurance:

Ordinary People, Extraordinary God

> *Lord, all my longing is known to thee,
>   my sighing is not hidden from thee.
> My heart throbs, my strength fails me;
>   and the light of my eyes — it also
>   has gone from me.*
>
> *But for thee, O Lord, do I wait;
>   it is thou, O Lord my God, who
>   wilt answer.*
>
> (Psalm 38:9-10, 15)

Leading as Loving

Proper 7   *2 Samuel 5:1-12*

Leadership is constantly being sought. The issue is neither academic nor boring because leadership is almost always pivotal. For this reason, schools, families, corporations, service clubs, governmental bodies are all perpetually in a search for capable leadership.

So is the church. Every year nominating committees in churches sit down and attempt to identify and enlist potential leaders. And that is a crucial task. The decisions they make can mean dynamic movement or inertia. I have been in churches where inept leadership has meant board meetings that drag on into the night; I have also been in churches where skilled leadership translated into meetings that covered immense ground within reasonable periods of time. If you have ever sat in on a trustee's meeting where half an hour was spent talking about whether or not to purchase a five dollar item, you know firsthand about the longing for gifted leadership.

Second Samuel's story of David's ascent to kingship is an important historical development in biblical history, but it is also a source of clues regarding the nature of effective leadership.

From the People

"We are your own flesh and blood," declare the tribes of Israel to David. (2 Samuel 5:1 TEV) Leadership with whom the people can identify makes all the difference in the world. There is something winsome about a president like Harry Truman who clearly was not affected by what he termed the "job" he had in Washington. His unassuming nature is reflected in some lines from Samuel Gallu's play, *Give 'em Hell Harry*. He has the President say,

> *I never saw myself as President. I was just in the right place at the wrong time. Lots of folks could do a better job, but it became mine to do, and as long as you put me here, you'll get the best I've got. I've always thought of myself as an ordinary man. I don't have any special endowments, and I don't waste time worrying about what I don't have. I just try to do the best with what I do have. I've always felt it's not important how you do something or say it; the point is to get it said and done.*

Occasionally producers have given us a movie centering around the theme of a runaway train. Initially, the engine is firmly linked to the cars it is pulling, but something like a jammed throttle enters the picture and the runaway engine is separated from the rest of the train and rushes headlong down the track toward certain disaster.

When leadership becomes radically disjointed from the body from which it has emerged, that also can be potentially disastrous. To lead does not mean to ride roughshod over, to insulate oneself from or to create a moat and pull up the drawbridge. Leadership listens and consults. When that does not happen, we begin to see events like the recent, and ultimately tragic, student revolt that rocked China.

Kurt Lewin extensively studied the dynamics of leadership and wrote about the "authoritarian" leader, the "laissez-faire" leader and the "democratic" leader. Alvin Lindgren, in summarizing Lewin's findings, wrote:

> *"Authoritarian" leadership evoked either a passive "rubber stamp" acceptance or hostile aggressive opposition. "Lasissez-faire" leadership likewise proved frustrating and ineffective, both in accomplishing the task of the group and in providing good internal relationships. The performance of the "democratic leader" was superior in task achievement and personal relationships as well.*
> (*Foundations for Purposeful Church Administration*, p. 168)

Over the years I have known ministers who have chosen to view their parishes as feudal estates over which they reign. The style of leadership they have embraced is of the authoritarian variety and the imprint of their own biases has been felt in every sector of congregational life, even including the kind of music a bride and groom should have for their wedding.

A good leader is always from the people, and to become insensitive to or forget that, is to take one giant step toward undermining one's own leadership.

A Covenant with the People

Leadership is also a covenant with the people. "He made a sacred alliance with them, they anointed him, and he became king of Israel." (2 Samuel 5:3 TEV) Specifically, it is a covenant to serve. Leadership linked to the purposes of

God is always an invitation to serve. Leaders do not see themselves as better or brighter than the led; rather, they view themselves as those with the gifts of organization and vision that enable them to lead a group from one point to another.

Years ago I distinctly remember being part of a large wedding party where the rehearsal was nothing short of a disaster. And if there is any place where you need a leader, it is at a wedding rehearsal! When that leadership is not present, the rehearsal can easily degenerate into a free-for-all akin to a square dance where a committee is calling the dance.

The officiating minister apparently came to the rehearsal minus a plan, and from start to finish it was a cacophonous mess. The mother of the bride would pull him in one direction, then a bridesmaid in another. In short order, they had him drawn and quartered, and what should have taken forty-five minutes, took nearly two hours.

It didn't need to be that way. There was no reason why the minister couldn't have organized the rehearsal in such a way that all could have been heard, with the responsibility for final decisions resting squarely upon the bride and groom. That's what leadership is all about — helping a group move from one point to another in a fair, well-oiled manner. To enable that is to serve. It is a gift always sorely needed in the body of Christ.

Involved with the People

"The time came when King David and his men set out. . . ." (2 Samuel 5:6 TEV) Too, leadership is a partnership in which both the leader and the led roll up their sleeves and get to work.

One dark evening I was having trouble finding an address and so pulled into an abandoned gas station, pulled a map out of the glove compartment, and tried to find it. As I was

Pentecost I

searching, a police car pulled up behind me. The officer asked if he could help; I explained my problem and he not only told me where to find the address, but indicated he would lead me directly to it.

That's a very simple illustration of involved leadership. A good leader delegates, but delegation does not mean abandonment or withdrawal.

Long before some of the creative Japanese managerial styles came to this country, I worked for a large corporation as a summer employee. In that company the pecking order was very clear. The folks to whom I reported were foremen and they in turn reported to a man who was called "the supervisor." The only time I had any significant contact with "the supervisor" was on an occasion when I had neglected to wear safety gloves, cut my hand, and was asked to discuss my transgression with "the supervisor." At least as we lower-level employees saw it, the supervisors were removed from the rank and file and that was even true during coffee breaks and lunch hours. They ate at one table and we ate at another.

Enlightened leadership, at least in the church if nowhere else, rubs elbows with anyone and everyone. Leadership is not a "from on high" proposition; it is a grass roots undertaking.

The story is told about an old man who promised to give each of his ten children 100 gold coins on the day of his death. It happened that as his death approached, his resources were less than he had hoped they would be. The first nine came forward, embraced their father and received 100 gold coins. When it came to the youngest son, the father asked the others to leave and said to the last son, "My son I have terrible news. Though I have been able to give each of your brothers and sisters 100 gold coins, I have but twenty for you." The youngest protested, "Father if you knew this, why did you not make adjustments with all of your children?"

The father responded, "It is better that I keep my word to as many as possible. Although I cannot give you as many gold coins as I promised, I can give you my greatest treasure. In addition to the twenty coins which I have for you, I offer you my ten closest companions. Their friendship is worth more than all the gold I have ever possessed. I urge you to treat them kindly." With that, the man died.

When the period of mourning had ended, the nine took extended vacations. The youngest remained home and was deeply disappointed. When the young man paid off his debts, he had only four coins left. Feeling obligated, he spent the last four on a dinner for his father's ten closest friends.

When the meal was over, the old men said to each other, "This is the only child who treats us with kindness. Let us return his affection."

The next day each of the ten sent two cattle and a small purse of money to the youngest son. Some of the old men provided assistance in breeding the cattle. Soon he had a huge herd. Others of the ten offered advice on investments. And it was not long before the youngest son had greater wealth than his nine siblings. Above his desk the young man wrote these words: "Friendship is of more value than gold." (William R. White. *Stories For Telling*, pp. 130-131) Good leadership works like that; it invests itself in those led and the process yields abundant fruit.

Accountable to God

The story of David's ascent to power ends with this comment, "He grew stronger all the time, because the Lord God Almighty was with him." (2 Samuel 5:10 TEV)

Accountability in leadership is absolutely essential. Accountability to those being led and to God. Very clearly God

Pentecost I

plays a significant role in David's leadership, and so must God in our leading, too.

It comes down, I think, to this: Wherever Christian people are leading — in the congregation, the university, the professional organization, or in elected political office — the question ever before them must be this: Will God, as I conceive of God, be pleased with the decisions and strategies I am employing, and will these further kingdom values?

Bayard Taylor, a poet from the last century, put it well:

> *Who, harnessed in his mail of Self, demands*
> *To be men's master and their sovereign guide?*
> *Proclaims his place, and by sole right of pride*
> *A candidate for love and reverence stands,*
> *As if the power within his empty hands*
> *Had fallen from the sky, with all beside,*
> *So oft to longing and to toil denied,*
> *That makes the leaders and the lords of lands?*
> *He who would lead must first himself be led;*
> *Who would be loved be capable to love*
> *Beyond the utmost he receives, who claims*
> *The rod of power must first have bowed*
> *And being honored, honor what's above:*
> *This know the men who leave the world their names.*
> (James Dalton Morrison, *Masterpieces of Religious Verse*, p. 303)

Leading is yet another manifestation of loving; it is a gift we employ in the service of our sisters and brothers.

An Untouchable God?

Proper 8   *2 Samuel 6:1-15*

The story of the ark's removal to Jerusalem is vintage Old Testament so far as most of us are concerned. It features a storm-and-battle God, fearful and yet rejoicing believers, and a great deal of religious uncertainty. Reading it from the vantage point of the latter years of the Twentieth Century, we are apt to question its relevance for our day. But let's not write it off with undue haste. We are never quite as sophisticated as we think we are and, inversely, the pioneers of faith are never quite as simple-minded as we might be led to believe.

Some Background

The ark, you will recall, was a representation of the presence of God. Writes Norman Gottwald, "The ark was a portable box, probably representing an imageless throne. It accompanied the Hebrews in their wanderings and went with them into battle." (*A Light To The Nations*, p. 143) It is

Ordinary People, Extraordinary God

the removal of this object by David to Jerusalem that sets the stage for this drama.

We need also to remember that whenever this ark was to be removed, there was a ritual associated with that removal. This ritual is described in Numbers 4. But what, specifically, we need to remember in understanding this intriguing drama from 2 Samuel is that the carrying of this ark was understood to be an exceedingly holy activity which, if not done according to the prescribed methods, would result in the death of any who violated those methods.

Describing the duties of the Levite clan of Kohat, the group charged with carrying the ark, two verses from Numbers 4 will give us a sense for the gravity that was to accompany the discharge of this responsibility:

> *Their service involves the most holy things.*
> (Numbers 4:4)
>
> *The Kohath clan must not touch the sacred objects, or they will die.*
> (Numbers 4:15)

The Unfolding Drama

David and a large company of people are dancing and singing as the ark is being moved along toward Jerusalem. Two chaps, Uzzah and Ahio, are guiding it along when the oxen pulling it stumble. Uzzah reaches out to steady the ark and suddenly dies. That death is attributed to God: "At once the Lord God became angry with Uzzah and killed him because of his irreverence." (2 Samuel 6:7 TEV)

Keeping in mind what we have said about the utter seriousness involved in moving the ark, place yourself in Uzzah's sandals for a moment. If you were told that the object you were going to move was tantamount to moving God, or

Pentecost I

the residence God inhabited, and if further you were told that under no circumstances were you to touch God's abode, and then, through no fault of your own, saw that abode beginning to fall to the ground and involuntarily reached out to steady it — as you would any other falling object — wouldn't that be for you an exceedingly charged moment? Uzzah probably had a heart attack. Severe shocks can do that to people; that's been documented.

A friend once showed me an envelope that was addressed by George Washington. His name was written on the front, and on the back of it he had written a message. My friend took it out of its protective shield and as I held it, I felt as though I had something very valuable in my hand and thought how tragic it would be were I to accidentally tear it or in some other way damage it. Indeed, it was valuable, many thousands of dollars valuable, and my friend indicated that were his father to need long-term nursing home care, the price fetched by this envelope would probably largely cover the cost of that care.

It was an unusual feeling to hold and touch that envelope, almost as though through it old George and I met. Magnify those feelings trillions of times and you can gain a sense of how Uzzah might have felt when he thought he had done the forbidden and virtually touched God!

His death, of course, is attributed to God. David becomes furious. The holy becomes too hot to handle and the ark is left along the roadside at the house of Obed Edom.

How often we are quick to place this interpretation on circumstances. Years back, a woman in one of my congregations came to me because she was troubled by the ill health of one of her children, a daughter. She had been thirty-seven when this daughter was born and the pregnancy was not a welcome one. As she tells it, her physician and friends denied her the right to her unhappy feelings. The physician told her the child would be a comfort to her in later years. The

Ordinary People, Extraordinary God

daughter developed a diabetic condition and this was naturally a source of worriment for the woman. But it was more than normal worriment.

It happened that this woman had a friend who also had a daughter when she was thirty-seven years old. This friend had not wanted to be pregnant either and at nineteen her daughter had died of leukemia, and it was her mother's contention that the child's death represented the punishment of God for the unhappy feelings she had about being pregnant nineteen years before. The woman in my congregation saw these as parallel circumstances and thought that her child would die, too, when she turned nineteen, again as punishment from God for not wanting to be pregnant with this daughter years before. What a tremendous — and I would add emphatically unnecessary — burden to carry.

You see, I think David was too quick to see the punishment of God in Uzzah's death, and often we are not different from our predecessors in faith. I don't think God killed Uzzah for trying to steady the ark; I think Uzzah died of fright over the belief that in some way he had violated God. And who of us, given the mind set of that day, would not have had a similar reaction?

One could certainly have a mental field day over the image of the ark off to the side of the road. In matters of faith, how often a man or woman comes to a point of discontentment and tables matters of faith, maybe even forever. How often a person of faith encounters doubt, and thinking doubt is chronic and not episodic, puts faith off to the side and lets it sit there. With what regularity people come to a point in congregational relationships where they are disgruntled and leave their churchmanship off to the side of the road! How frequently we encounter something that troubles us and let it sit on the side of the road, pretending it away.

After a time, David hears that the ark has not been a source of trouble, but instead a blessing for Obed Edom's

Pentecost I

family, and so determines to continue with his efforts to get it to Jerusalem. Initially, David is extremely guarded and cautious. Wouldn't we be, too? "After the men carrying the Covenant Box had gone six steps, David had them stop while he offered the Lord a sacrifice of a bull and a fatted calf." (2 Samuel 6:13 TEV) David wasn't about to take any chances. If God had any feelings about the ark of his presence being moved any further, David wanted to know about them. But nothing happened after six steps.

We can understand the caution. If an athlete hurts herself by over-extending, she is going to be cautious when normal activity is resumed. If we fail in one marriage, we are going to go (or at least should go) more slowly into the next one. Should the declaration of our feelings meet with rebuff from some quarter of our lives, then at least in that quarter we will disclose more slowly the next time.

But we can also understand the joy and dancing! What a relief that the Lord God was going to allow the movement of the ark to continue. Despite the proclivity of David and company to erroneously see God's hand in Uzzah's death, they can still become celebrative over their reclaimed understanding that God has blessed their plan. "David, wearing only a linen cloth around his waist, danced with all his might to honor the Lord. And so he and all the Israelites took the Covenant Box up to Jerusalem with shouts of joy and the sound of trumpets." (2 Samuel 6:14-15 TEV)

Our worship should always in part be dance. I don't mean that folks ought to get out of their pews and start to dance about at will whenever they feel so moved, although intentional liturgical dance can be a beautiful expression of faith. But I do mean that there ought to be a dance-like quality about our singing and other expressions of corporate worship. There is no reason why a responsive reading or litany cannot be an expression of joy and praise; they are intended to be infinitely more than liturgical droanings through which one must pass in order to get to the meat which is the sermon.

The Good News Bible (Today's English Version) is full of little pencil sketches that help capture the moods and insights of the Bible. Check out, sometime, the sketch that is attendant to this drama from the sixth chapter of 2 Samuel. It very clearly and delightfully depicts what it means for God's people to rejoice.

A Story Completed Later

So our drama ends on a joyful note. The ark arrives safely in Jerusalem. But it leaves us with the impression that God is almost untouchable; and if not untouchable, touchable only when God wants to be touched.

That issue is addressed fully and forever later in the New Testament and in no place there more poignantly than in the story of the woman who suffered with a severe bleeding disorder, related in all the synoptic gospels. (Mark 5, Matthew 9 & Luke 8) This woman's alleged uncleanness removed her from the consolations of faith (see Leviticus 15); it was held that her condition rendered her unacceptable to God.

Little wonder that when she heard of Jesus and his healing ways, her hope was rekindled. Maybe this was one from the religious community who would not hold her at arm's length and make her feel unworthy. Perchance here was one from God whom she could reach out and actually touch. And she does. And she improves. And Jesus accepts and even affirms what it must have taken great courage for her to do. "My daughter, your faith has made you well. Go in peace, and be healed of your trouble." (Mark 5:34 TEV) Here is one, unlike Uzzah, who reaches out and intentionally touches him who is God, and far from killing her, it heals and restores her — a long way from our story in 2 Samuel.

Pentecost I

The good news of the Gospel? God can be touched and confidently so. Or perhaps more true to the Gospel story, God reaches out and touches us in Christ Jesus redemptively and gracefully and says, "Don't be afraid of my touch. It is a healing touch and it is for your salvation."

A Sleeping Bag God

Proper 9   *2 Samuel 7:1-17*

This is definitely not a text a minister should use if her congregation is thinking of building a new church structure or adding to an existing one. King David, well-meaning to be sure, develops pangs of conscience because he is living in his "house built of cedar" and thinks to do better by God. "Here I am living in a house built of cedar, but God's Covenant Box is kept in a tent!" (2 Samuel 7:2 TEV) So David determines to build God a temple, and initially with the prophet, Nathan's, blessing.

Misreading God

It is obviously all too easy to misread what God wants. But that is really no surprise, because often we do not do well in reading what another person really wants, either. We offer one thing, and what they want is something quite different. We offer what we think they want and what they need is light-years away. A husband offers something material, but his wife is hoping for a gift from the heart. A parent offers a child money or toys, but the child wants not gift, but parent.

Paul Tournier, in *The Meaning of Gifts*, tells of a husband who had a collection of pipes. Each time his wife had a birthday, he would offer her a pipe "to enrich the collection." For an unknown reason, her husband finally caught on to the truth that all those pipes were for him and not his wife. The wife remarked, "Just imagine, I just had my birthday and my husband bought me a bottle of perfume. I don't know what has come over him." (p. 17)

Little surprise, then, that we do the same with God. Throughout the history of the church we have known, thanks to Micah, that God doesn't want burnt calves, thousands of sheep, nor endless streams of olive oil. Those items change with every generation, but we still persist in offering God their correlatives, leaving justice, constant love, and true community virtually to chance.

Were Micah writing in our day, how might those words be expressed? Maybe in some fashion such as this: What shall we bring to the Lord, the God of heaven, to worship him? Shall we bring costly religious productions, carefully choreographed and videotaped, and at least put out on local cable stations? Shall we bring carefully coiffured people of faith who are of one mind on matters of doctrine, holding that its lowest common denominator is infinitely more preferential than spirited debate and the growth that can ensue from it? Shall we bring before the Lord our fawning and falderol and not, instead, our honest humanity, pimples and all?

No House for God

God doesn't want to live in a house; that God makes clear to David through Nathan. "From the time I rescued the

Pentecost I

people of Israel from Egypt until now, I have never lived in a temple; I have traveled around living in a tent." (2 Samuel 7:6 TEV)

God is disclosed not as a domesticated, but instead as a dynamic God. God cannot be cabined and caught; harnessed and held; isolated and studied. No. God is too busy for that. God is constantly on the move with his people, seen now in this event and later in quite another guise. God rejects the suggestion that he can be placed here or there, or that he can be the object of a definitive analysis. As confident as we are that God has disclosed himself in Christ Jesus, there is still truth in the words of Isaiah:

For my thoughts are not your thoughts,
neither are your ways my ways, says the Lord.
For as the heavens are higher than the earth,
so are my ways higher than your ways
and my thoughts than your thoughts.
(Isaiah 55:8-9)

This story serves to remind us just how often we try, and inaccurately so, to pigeonhole and second-guess.

One thinks of the women's movement and how once we had a very restricted and truncated sense of who women were and what they could do. In the not-so-distant past it was not uncommon for people to make derogatory comments about females in the pulpit, for example. However, more and more people are coming to realize that women clergy can be quite effective in the pulpit, as well as in other pastoral roles.

Inversely, we have also tried to pigeonhole males. There is no good reason why a man cannot be as at home in the kitchen as a woman. To hold that women are better at changing diapers than men is silly and untrue.

In religion, and likewise in politics, we want to think of people in terms of labels. We want to call them liberals or conservatives, when it is infinitely more true that we are all a mix of both. On some counts we are liberal; on others, conservative.

Then clearly we sometimes pigeonhole ourselves. We set the parameters of our lives too close at hand, thinking we can never do or be something beyond those parameters. Then something happens in our lives and we — as the saying goes — "rise above" ourselves. We can all think of people who are doing today what they never could have envisioned themselves doing a decade ago.

Recently I had occasion to visit with old friends. When I had lived next door to these people, Mary was a rather diminutive mother of three girls. She scarcely raised her voice at them, let alone raised it for any other reason. That was fourteen years ago, and today, she runs her own day care center and in that capacity relates to a wide variety of people and circumstances in ways that she never dreamed possible fourteen years prior.

But we also pigeonhole and limit theologically.

We do that with our faith. Some treat religious doctrines and ideas as though they are cast in cement, as though they are destinations, and not vehicles of conveyance to the truth. And in this there is real danger.

For instance, a public school teacher we once knew appeared to be the very embodiment of boredom and uselessness. That proved to be a hasty conclusion. For over the months and years that followed our introduction to this person, this seemingly ineffectual teacher came to distinguish himself in a variety of ways. Our initial impression, informed though it was by an episode or two, proved to be an inaccurate one. It would have been unfair for us to hold to that notion when evidence to the contrary became consistently clear.

So, too, should it be with our religious ideas. They should always be tentatively held, pending the disclosure of future insight.

Pentecost I

I submit that this, not a frenzied defense of orthodoxy, is the essence of trust. Such a stance is informed also by the joyful conviction that God continues to reveal truth to his children. We worship not an idea about God, but God, and it is our encounters with God and God's grace that should shape our notions. It is not our notions about God that should place us in the posture of second-guessing what our encounter with God is going to be like.

Eric Hoffer's book *The True Believer* is about fanaticism, and he describes the fanatic in these terms:

> *To be in possession of an absolute truth is to have a net of familiarity spread over the whole of eternity. There are no surprises and no unknowns. All questions have already been answered, all decisions made, all eventualities foreseen. The true believer is without wonder and hesitation.*
> (p. 71)

Religious people can take on those characteristics, and when they do, how sad and indeed faithless it is to worship a God with whom there are no unknowns and surprises and no wonder.

Then, too, we try to pigeonhole God, give God a specific place, and expect that God will be there and not somewhere else. I suppose that the most common example of this would be the expectation that God dwells in buildings we refer to as churches and perhaps at most makes guest appearances elsewhere. But God, as our story from Second Samuel discloses, will not allow himself to be so relegated. Sure, God is in his holy temples, but God also carries the temple of his presence into the near and far-off places. The surgical suite can be the temple of his presence, as can the kindergarten room or the production line. God can come like the unassuming presence of a beloved friend, but God can just as surely come as one from a far-off place who stands over against us.

Ordinary People, Extraordinary God

Frederick Buechner has described it beautifully when he writes of his decision to embrace a ministry of writing on a mountain in western Vermont:

> *I discovered that if you really keep your eye peeled to it and your ears open, if you really pay attention to it, even such a limited and limiting life as the one I was living on Rupert Mountain opened up onto extraordinary vistas . . . There is no event too commonplace but that God is present within it, always hiddenly, always leaving you room to recognize him or not to recognize him, but all the more fascinatingly because of that, all the more compellingly and hauntingly.*
>
> (*Now & Then*, p. 87)

God the House Builder

Our story begins with David wanting to build a house for God, but it ends ironically with God reminding David that God will continue to move for the establishment of David and his people: "I have gone with you wherever you have gone. . . . I have chosen a place for my people Israel . . . I promise to keep you safe . . . I will withdraw my support." (2 Samuel 7:9-16) Those are words of establishment.

Often in our work with people who have for some period been absent from the institutional church, we will hear them say, "I have to get back to church." Often implied is, "I've got to get back to God," too. People do forget God. For a time, sometimes a long time, they don't think about God, pray to God, or wonder about God. But the wonderful news of the Bible, illustrated by this story, is that God doesn't forget us. God is always an establishing God, at work whether we acknowledge that work or not, tireless in his efforts to lead us through our wildernesses into lands of milk and honey.

Pentecost I

God is, we might say, a sleeping bag God in the sense that his residence is not in one place, but in all places at all times, recognized or not, rebuffed or not, always working for the good of his people. God, our story declares, is a moving and dynamic God, out always among his people wherever their travels take them. And God is a sleeping bag God not in the sense that he sleeps as we sleep, but in the sense that he travels lightly to better serve the needs of his children.

So the psalmist's words of praise are also ours:

The protector of Israel
*   never dozes or sleeps.*
The Lord will guard you;
*   he is by your side to protect*
*   you.*
The sun will not hurt you during
*   the day,*
nor the moon during the night.

The Lord will protect you from
*   all danger;*
*   he will keep you safe.*
He will protect you as you come
*   and go*
*   now and forever.*

(Psalm 121:4-8 TEV)

A Thanksgiving Checklist

Proper 10   *2 Samuel 7:18-29*

Do you ever find yourself getting confused over actual holidays and legal holidays? I do. About all that I am ever really sure of is that holidays mean sales. In fact, I am convinced that if you were to take certain holidays and ask the person on the street how we came to have them and what they mean, the majority wouldn't have the foggiest. Pulaski? Who's Pulaski?

In 1927 Reinhold Niebuhr noted how Thanksgiving can become twisted and wrested from its germinal essence. He wrote:

> *Thanksgiving becomes increasingly the business of congratulating the Almighty upon his most excellent co-workers, ourselves. It would be better to strut unashamedly down the boardwalk of nations than to go through the business of bowing before God while we say, 'We thank thee Lord that we are not as other men.'*
> (*Leaves From The Notebook of a Tamed Cynic*, pp. 173-174)

Ordinary People, Extraordinary God

Hence, it becomes alarmingly easy to pass right through a time of celebration like Thanksgiving and never really be grasped by its abiding significance.

For Christians, it is clear that gratitude is the very heartbeat of the biblical drama. Whether one is reading in the New or Old Testament, one is constantly confronted with words of gratitude and praise. Perhaps to re-read portions of the Bible that concern themselves with gratitude is a sure way of wresting Thanksgiving from its secular expressions. There is an authenticity and freshness about hearing from men and women whose life passages have flooded their lives with gratefulness. For instance, David's expression in the seventh chapter of 2 Samuel. "How great you are, Sovereign Lord! There is none like you; we have always known that you alone are God!" (2 Samuel 7:22 TEV)

By way of rescuing Thanksgiving from our department stores and insuring that this holiday can be an affair of the heart for us all, consider this Thanksgiving checklist:

Checklist item #1: Am I remembering to say thank-you? Some may maintain that this item is for elementary school children, and I would agree. It is. But often we find adults acting like children; adults need to be reminded that the verbal expressions of gratitude are important.

On one level the expression of thanksgiving can be seen as a matter of manners, and manners are more essential than optional. Manners are to human intercourse what glue is to model building — try to get along without them and things begin to fall apart. Without manners we would have the regrettable spectacle of people who interrupt without apology, request without grace, receive without acknowledgment, and inquire without tact.

On another level, "thank-you" is an acknowledgment of helpfulness. "Thank-you" is a verbal recognition to another that they have well served us. It affirms what they have done and encourages them to do more of it. Our appreciation becomes their inspiration.

Pentecost I

And on still another level, the ability to say "thank-you" separates the human being from the parasite. One who is legitimately grateful is not usually found to be one who arrogantly presumes and parasitically lives off the kindness of other people.

Every group seems to have at least one individual who functions out of what I call the vacuum cleaner syndrome. That is to say, this individual, just like your Hoover or Electrolux or Kirby, laps up everything with which he comes into contact. He laps up all the attention, all the support, all the concern, and all the caring he possibly can and never does he turn back to say "thank-you." No matter how he works the ledger, he always seems to come up with more liabilities than assets, and so goes off again and again in search of more to consume.

The author of Hebrews knew people like that and remarks to them in the fifth chapter of that letter, ". . . by this time you ought to be teachers . . ." (Hebrews 5:12) Apparently these folks have been "taking in" for years and years and still are, even though by this time they should be "putting out."

Checklist item #2: Do I realize that I am never out of debt? That's not a financial statement, but it is a spiritual and an emotional one. It is the psalmist declaring, "Hear my cry, O Lord; listen to my call for help! If you kept a record of our sins, who could escape being condemned? But you forgive us, so that we should reverently obey you." (Psalm 130:2-4 TEV)

Think of the whole host of people through whose efforts we are ushered into adulthood. Even when there have been rotten apples in the family barrel, one still cannot dismiss the important others in our lives, and often they have been myriad: mother, father, siblings, neighbors, teachers, friends, ministers, aunts, uncles, and the list goes on. This is to say

Ordinary People, Extraordinary God

nothing about the infrastructure of community, state, and nation and the goods and services we take for granted.

Checklist item #3: Does my selfishness set the trigger of gratitude too low? When we are born, we are born turned in on ourselves; it could be no other way. Over the course of human development we gradually become aware of others around us and move from the center of the circle to a place, with others, along the edge of the circle. However, sometimes, for various reasons, we fail to make that total journey from the center of the circle to a point along its edge. When that happens, we center too much attention on ourselves and evidence "entitlement behavior." We come to feel that we are due this or due that. This should not be confused with affirming our basic human rights. Rather it has to do with the feeling that we are entitled to special treatment. And if that is our feeling, it is probable that we will set the trigger of gratitude far too low. Our demands on others will be so extraordinary, that few will and should comply; but from our perspective there will be little reason to say "thank you."

I am reminded of a transient who came to me wanting help with food. I discovered he was already staying at our local shelter and had food vouchers for a very fine local restaurant, but he complained of not liking the food at either place and wanted me to provide him with funds so that he could eat elsewhere. That's entitlement, and a person with that mind set is not apt to say "thank you" often, if at all.

Checklist item #4: Is my thanksgiving being translated into generosity? Thanksgiving that is genuine has a motivating power behind it. It makes us want to get up and do something for someone else. And to spur us along in that direction there is a gospel one-liner that should be remembered and read aloud after every Thanksgiving dinner: "Everyone to whom much is given, of him will much be required . . ." (Luke 12:48)

It is the psalmist, then, who raises the correct question: "What shall I render to the Lord for all his bounty to me?" (Psalm 116:12)

Having received, we give; having been blessed, we bless; having been forgiven, we forgive; having been liberated, we liberate.

We all see this dynamic illustrated in many ways, but I remember hearing of a seminary professor in Rochester, New York, who funded an undergraduate program for several young people. It happened that a cousin of mine was helped by this man. I never heard the professor's story, but I suspect that if I had, it would have been along lines of the biblical mandate that having received, we are asked to give.

Checklist item #5: Do I see myself as a child of God to whom my wonder is a sacrifice of thanksgiving? Clearly there is wonderment in David's prayer of thanksgiving when he speaks of God having "made this wonderful promise to me." (2 Samuel 7:28 TEV)

Not that everything in the world is wonderful; it isn't. Only a Pollyanna could believe that. Yet our ability to see the wonder-full around us is to place before God our sacrifice of thanksgiving. Full of wonder is a blazing hearth before us; full of wonder is the little child snuggled in its mother's arms; full of wonder is a father extending himself to a needful son or daughter; full of wonder is the emerging sunrise and the receding sunset; full of wonder is the ability to free someone with a word; and full of wonder is that sense of knowing that defies analysis. Wonder translates into praise and becomes our sacrifice of thanksgiving to the One in whose image we have been created.

Culturally, thanksgiving has become a holiday. But for those who understand its deeper dimensions, it is — more to the point — a holy day.

David and the Devil

Proper 11   *2 Samuel 11:1-15*

We can be thankful that the Bible is brutally honest about the people whose stories it tells. Because of this, we are able to see the power of God at work in the lives of very human people. What's more, if this were not the case and instead the Bible whitewashed its personalities, we would begin to wonder whether it seriously addressed the very real brokenness and moral failures that can mark all our lives.

No question about it, the story of David and Bathsheba is an exceedingly human story. It easily qualifies as biblical soap opera. Alter it but slightly, and what it describes goes on all the time. When these circumstances are replayed in the life of a public official, we are apt to hear all the lurid details for days in the press. And when they are replayed in the life of a public religious figure, like Jim Bakker or Jimmy Swaggart, we are apt to hear about them for months on end.

A Common Scenario

The opening scenes of our biblical drama are certainly not uncommon. "One day, late in the afternoon, David got up from his nap (I wonder what he might have been dreaming about?) and went to the palace roof. As he walked around up there, he saw a woman taking a bath in her house. She was very beautiful." (2 Samuel 11:2) Nothing oblique yet. Every day, women and men encounter people of the opposite sex whose physical countenance leads them to give pause. To themselves, at least, they acknowledge an attraction. But that's all there is to it. They don't bid goodbye to spouse and children and go off in pursuit of this source of attraction. At least not most of the time, although many of us are painfully aware of the exceptions.

A Deadly Turn

But David is one of those exceptions. "So he sent a messenger to find out who she was . . ." (2 Samuel 11:3) And then, "David sent messengers to get her . . ." (2 Samuel 11:4)

If we could crawl inside the mind and heart of David on that rooftop, what do you suppose we would find? What buttons got pushed that led to his obliquity? What happened on the inside that led David from chance beholding to planned inappropriateness? After all, he didn't have to act on what he saw. Most people, even though they could steal a Rolex without ever being discovered, wouldn't do it; but a few would. Where is the difference? Why do you suppose that's so?

There are probably many reasons, but let me reach into the tradition of the church and talk about David capitulating to the Devil. I do that with some trepidation, because it is tragically easy to fall into the Flip Wilson mode and say,

Pentecost I

"The Devil made me do it," and thus avoid any sense of personal responsibility. But I take the figure of the Devil to be a very animated way of talking about the presence of evil within human personality, and on that basis, I propose that we bring the Devil into our considerations. Clearly, David capitulated to that evil, to the Devil, when he moved from chance beholding to the acting out of his feelings. And the point is this: he didn't have to do that. He could have argued and struggled and fought with the Devil, even as Jesus later in the Bible struggles with the Devil.

This was a deadly turn because it spelled trouble for all affected by it.

It meant trouble for David because it really didn't get him what he wanted. The Devil convinced David that Bathsheba would in some way complete him, but that was not so.

There is a story about a prince who searched near and far for a beautiful woman to be his princess and fulfull his life. By chance (isn't that just how it happened to David?) he noticed a young woman whose beauty drew forth intense romantic and joyful feelings from his heart. He thought of her day and night. He said to himself, "I cannot live without her." He wrote poems, composed songs, brought her treasures, kissed her hand, fought off other princes, but could not convince her to marry him.

His counsel of wisemen met and said, "Oh prince, you have become so sad with love you cannot do your daily duties. You must win her love or give her up. For it is worse to have a lovesick prince who has no wife, than an able prince who has no wife." The prince replied, "She is everything to me, I cannot live without her. I must win her or die."

The prince's persistence paid off and the beautiful woman consented to become his princess. The prince was ecstatic. His mind began to create all kinds of beautiful images and stories; scenes of everlasting romantic bliss, happiness surrounded by children, triumphs applauded by his kingdom. The prince, the wisemen, and the whole kingdom celebrated a week-long festival and wedding.

Once married, the wisemen noticed the prince seemed troubled, disorganized, unable to eat or sleep. They asked him what was wrong. He replied, "Three things torture me. First, whereas before I could not keep from thinking I must have her love or I cannot live, now I cannot stop thinking that if I lose her love, I cannot live. Second, the more I pursue her the more she wants to get away; she has created a separate territory in the castle for herself. Third, she has grown cold; the flame of my love cannot warm the dungeon of her heart."

Just so with David. The Devil duped David into thinking that Bathsheba was the answer to all his problems. Wrong, David!

But David's acting out also meant problems for Bathsheba. We don't know whether she was a willing participant or not. One cannot dismiss out of hand the special pressure she must have felt, given the source of the demand upon her. Then there is the resultant pregnancy, and it is plausible that it was an unwelcome pregnancy for her. We have no way of knowing. But we do know that David's capitulation to the Devil certainly involved a major fallout for Bathsheba.

Then there is Uriah. The cost to him was death. At first David tried to engineer matters so that it would look like the child was Uriah's. But when that failed, he engineered Uriah's death. It was an exceedingly dark chapter in David's life.

So the dark turn meant big trouble for David and even greater trouble for others. Which is what happens when people take advantage of their positions, whether it is a minister in his parish, a teacher in her classroom, or a Wall Street stockbroker who becomes an inside trader. When we become the Devil's person, others get hurt, too.

Pentecost I

The Lesson

The lessons in all this?

First, the Devil is close at hand. For all of us. That's true whether it is a young child who grows comfortable with lying or an adult who emotionally and/or sexually abuses a child. James Hillman has written a word that must reach our ears: "The Devil's power seems to grow not in our shadow but from our light. He gains when we lose touch with our own darkness, when we lose sight of our own destructiveness and self-deceptions." (*Insearch: Psychology and Religion*, p. 91)

Second, the Devil is a strange bird. Speak up to him, say "no," and you'll be surprised how recessive he becomes. This happens when we help our children develop a healthy sense of conscience and when we impart positive values.

Recent research indicates that concern for others begins much earlier than we once thought. Studies show that almost at birth babies respond empathetically to the cries of another infant. Therefore it would seem that there is almost a kind of predisposition on the part of very young children that can be enhanced and encouraged or allowed to fade and die off.

A recent report sums it up like this: "Researchers have found that an active sense of social responsibility — behaving helpfully and cooperatively, for example — is unlikely to take root under parents who are either loosely permissive or strongly dictatorial. Parents who can integrate the best of both styles, combining firm authority with warmth and clear communication, seem most successful in planting the seeds of concern and thoughtfulness toward others." (*U.S. News & World Report*, November 21, 1988, p. 68)

Hope for David

We tend, it would seem, to see people in black and white terms. They are good or bad. But David reminds us that the matter is infinitely more complex.

His lack of struggle with the Devil meant that others got hurt, and hurt seriously. But David was not without his laudable side. His early life was filled with honor; he was a courageous warrior; he was politically shrewd and astute; he was a gifted musician; and he was a fine organizer. But he had his Achilles' heel and knew how to sew dragon's teeth.

Here, however, was David's hope: God wasn't finished with him yet! But that's a story for another day.

Speaking Truth to Power: The Ministry of Nathan

Proper 12   *2 Samuel 12:1-14*

In the wake of David's affair with Bathsheba, God was not content to let matters lie, and it fell to the prophet Nathan to be God's living word to David.

A Horrendous Task

How about it? Would you want to have been Nathan? When he realized what it was that God wanted him to do, it must have inaugurated more than a few anxiety attacks. I know it would have for me. Not that kings should be given that kind of power, or in fact have that kind of power, or even on the inside, feel they have that kind of power. However, we often attribute such power to them and act deferentially, whether that king is mother, father, boss, professor or whomever.

Still for most of us, talking to the king is a knee-knocking business unless we happen to be Barbara Walters. And it is even more knee-knocking when we have an unpleasant message for the king.

Ordinary People, Extraordinary God

A Resourceful Prophet

But Nathan was a resourceful prophet and locked onto the king without the king even knowing it. He told the king a simple, but moving, story.

There is an old Jewish tale about a rabbi who answered every question with a story. One day he was asked by a student, "Rabbi, you have a wonderful ability to select just the right story for each question. What, may I ask, is your secret?"

He smiled impishly and replied, "That reminds me of a story:" Once a young soldier was traveling through the countryside, when he stopped to rest his horse in a small hamlet. Walking about, he spied a wood fence, and on the wood fence were nearly forty small chalk circles, and right in the center of each was a bullet hole.

What incredulous accuracy, the soldier thought as he examined the fence. There isn't a single shot that has failed to hit the bulls-eye.

The soldier set out to discover the identity of the sharpshooter and was told it was a young boy.

"Who taught you to shoot so well?" the soldier asked.

"I taught myself," the young lad replied.

Not yet satisfied, the soldier pressed the boy further, "To what do you attribute your great skill?"

"Actually," began the lad, "it isn't very difficult. First I shoot at the fence, and then I take a piece of chalk and draw circles around the holes."

The rabbi chuckled for a moment, "Now you know my secret. I don't look for a story to answer a question. I collect every good story or parable I hear and then store it in my mind. When the right occasion or question arises, I point the story in its direction. In effect, I simply draw a circle around a hole that is already there." (William R. White, *Stories For the Journey*, p. 30)

Pentecost I

Basically, this is what Nathan did. Reaching into the recesses of his mind, he pointed a story in the direction of the king.

And what a story it was! A poor man and his family had a lamb, and it was a beloved pet. In fact, when the poor man's family was gathered for a meal, the lamb would sit on the poor man's lap and even eat table food. Maybe the family even gave the animal a name. And maybe, too, when the impoverished man had a bad day — and he probably had many of them — it almost seemed to him that the lamb understood. Its warmth comforted him. And its sounds had almost a hypnotic effect on him.

In that same town was a rich man and he had hundreds of cattle and sheep. Yet when a guest came to his home, he went and stripped this poor man and his family of their only pet, killed it, and served it to his guest because he didn't want to kill one of his own.

Think of a household pet that is or has been in your life, and you can readily gain a sense for the cruelness of what this rich man did. Can you imagine the pure cruelness, the unadulterated meanness of this man?

The story must certainly hit the bulls-eye with King David, because it instantaneously aroused his indignation. "I swear by the living Lord that the man who did this ought to die." (2 Samuel 12:5 TEV) It summoned his passion for capital punishment, and for justice. "For having done such a cruel thing, he must pay back four times as much as he took." (2 Samuel 12:6 TEV)

The Connectional Confrontation

You may remember that back in 1967 Lyndon Johnson met Alexei Kosygin (one of the reigning triumvirate that replaced Nikita Khrushchev as head of the USSR) in Glassboro, New Jersey, for a summit meeting. Hugh Sidey has said that Lyndon Johnson devised an elaborate form of body language in order to convince the Soviet leader that he was dealing with a tough Texas hombre. He gave him one of his crusher handshakes and also hovered over the significantly shorter man. Convinced that eye contact was a measure of a man's determination, Johnson locked eyes with Kosygin at one crucial point in their talks. Wanting a sip of coffee, L. B. J. felt for his cup of coffee on the table rather than release his visual grip on Kosygin, who finally blinked and looked away. Johnson thought that singular human triumph was important.

Maybe that's the way it was that day between Nathan and King David when Nathan connected the story of a rich and poor man to the king himself. Imagine this: the king's indignation has been fully touched — he readily identifies with the poor man in the story — when, perhaps eyeball-to-eyeball like L. B. J. and Kosygin, Nathan makes the connection between the story and the king. "You are that man. And this is what the Lord God of Israel says: 'I made you king of Israel and rescued you from Saul. I gave you his kingdom and his wives; I made you king over Israel and Judah. If this had not been enough, I would have given you twice as much. Why, then, have you disobeyed my commands? Why did you do this evil thing? You had Uriah killed in battle; you let the Ammonites kill him, and then you took his wife!' " (2 Samuel 12:7-9 TEV)

Speaking Truth To Power

Nathan speaks truth to power and, amazingly, the king listens. The story, and the king's response to it, have already set the stage. It hits him squarely between the eyes, and he can do nothing else but admit to the truth of what Nathan is saying. He is that man. And he has needed to know that

Pentecost I

because truth, in addition to its often stinging and burning characteristics, has a liberating quality.

The little girl I have in mind got caught in a lie. The person who blew the whistle on her left the matter in her lap. She now knew that someone else knew she had misrepresented a matter and it remained for her to make the next move. Next day she did. She was driving down the road with her parents when she suddenly burst into tears. Dad pulled over, her parents heard her confession of the stinging and burning truth, but the little girl also began to breathe much easier and felt liberated from the dark secret she had been keeping.

It's a banner day for the soul when it purges itself of darkness. "I have sinned against the Lord." (2 Samuel 12:13 TEV)

Today's Kings

This isn't just a story from a day long gone; it is also a summons to you and me to speak truth to power in our day. Where and who are the kings? They are everywhere. They show up in different places all the time. Kingliness has not been shed somewhere back in the mists of time. The faces of the autocratic can be single or collective; they can be found in board rooms and around kitchen tables; they can be young or they can be old; they can be in the government or in the private sector. But they are here and they are always sorely in need of the truth. And what truth? The truth that there is another king to whom they must be accountable, a king whose priorities and hopes are often far different from theirs.

Walter Bruggemann has said of this king:

He is a God uncredentialed in the empire, unknown in the courts, unwelcome in the temple. And his history begins in his attentiveness to the cries of the marginal ones. . . . caring, weeping, grieving, and rejoicing will not be outflanked by royal hardware or royal immunity because this one indeed is God. And kings must face that.
(*The Prophetic Imagination*, p. 42)

Hope for Kings

King David did a despicable thing. It was wrong, sinful, and displeasing to God. But his soul moved from the darkness of midnight nearer first light when he confessed, "I have sinned against the Lord." Because of this, Nathan has this word for the king from God: "The Lord forgives you; you will not die." (2 Samuel 12:14 TEV)

Even autocrats, wherever they are found and whoever they are, can be forgiven. As God sees the matter, it is never too late in the day for the most mean and the most cruel to feel the blessings of grace. Not a cheap grace, mind you, but a grace cognizant of the great wrong that has been done, a grace whose zeal is fueled by sincere penitence, and a grace that can turn the most twisted but willing heart toward the light of the Kingdom.

It is a strange notion to many of us. People do some heinous things to other people. But when all is said and done, the matter rests with God, who says to us, as Isaiah puts the matter, "For my thoughts are not your thoughts, neither are your ways my ways, says the Lord." (Isaiah 55:8) And in that is our hope. Thanks be to God!

When Matters Hang in the Balance

Proper 13 2 Samuel 12:15b-24

When our son was very small, he developed a strange disorder that manifested itself in an excruciating pain that roamed from joint to joint. It would be in one elbow, then the other; it would then move on to a knee and so forth. As part of the diagnostic procedures, he was given an EKG, and I still have a very vivid mental picture of the little fellow all wired and lying on a hospital bed. Our anxiety was heightened by the fact that for a time, the medical people could not arrive at any definite diagnosis. We were told that it might be necessary to admit Matthew to a Boston hospital specializing in pediatric medicine. For a time, matters hung in the balance.

When matters hang in the balance, we hang in the balance with them. And it can be a torturous business to be so suspended.

Hanging in the balance could easily describe what happened to David in this episode from 2 Samuel. David had repented of his sin involving Bathsheba, but a heavy matter remained and that was the illness and probable death of the child born of their imprudence.

Ordinary People, Extraordinary God

Bad Theology

Greatly troublesome is the first verse from this episode in David's life: "The Lord caused the child that Uriah's wife had borne to David to become very sick." (2 Samuel 12:15b TEV) "The Lord caused . . ." This Old Testament notion is laid to rest in the New Testament, but it continues to linger, if not as true, at least as possible in the minds of modern people. Listen closely and you will find people who believe, or at least consider the notion, that their illness is punishment from God for sin. More than once people have raised that issue with me as their pastor. But this is bad — no sick — theology. It's my impression that Old Testament thinkers and writers read this into the stories of these people. I have no problem immediately rejecting such notions out of hand.

For instance, Jesus responded to the disciples' query about a man born blind, "Teacher, whose sin caused him to be born blind? Was it his own or his parents' sin?" And Jesus replies, "His blindness has nothing to do with his sins or his parents' sins." (John 9:2-3 TEV)

The essence of what Leslie Weatherhead once said to parents grief-stricken over the untimely death of their little son in a cholera epidemic must be lifted up any time we hear people assuming that tragedy is the will of God: "Call your little boy's death the result of mass ignorance, call it mass folly, call it mass sin, if you like, call it bad drains or communal carelessness, but don't call it the will of God." (*The Will of God*, p. 11)

Eating the Bread of Anxious Toil

Clearly our story pictures David as one who is, to borrow a phrase from the 127th Psalm, "eating the bread of anxious toil." Doesn't that well describe the interior state of

Pentecost I

people who are waiting while matters hang in the balance? It is a time to be upset, and there is no value in trying to deny or hide that condition. To the contrary, there is value in admitting that we are extremely upset and worried. What is disclosed can be handled; what is hidden confounds us.

Years ago a small group of us were huddled together in a hospital waiting room just off a cardiac care unit (and waiting rooms like that are always places where matters are hanging in the balance). Grammy Barber's life was hanging in the balance, and I had joined some of her children in their vigil. She was their beloved mother, but she was a beloved friend of our family, too. We talked and wondered and prayed and fretted, and then we heard that ominous code over the loudspeaker summoning all available medical personnel to the cardiac unit. Was it Grammy? We wondered.

When the family physician came into view, we knew the answer to our question. It was Grammy, and for a time we continued to be upset people.

There is no getting around the fact that life will at times hang in the balance for us. Just like David, we will reject food, pray to God, maintain our nocturnal vigils and cope as best we can.

What will we want from others at times like that? David's court officials wanted him to get up, perhaps go out and get something to eat, get some fresh air, and clean up a bit. He resisted. While different people will require different treatment, if there is any principle that can be operative here, it is the principle that folks have a right to grapple with matters in a style that is theirs. Maybe it's not the way we would do it, but it is their way and provided it isn't fundamentally injurious to them or others, it is to be honored. And we are to be there listening, supporting, reflecting or, as we say in the church, ministering.

We have friends whose daughter, at a very early age, contracted leukemia. Luckily, she had a physician who quickly diagnosed her and she was sent immediately to Roswell Park for treatment. Chemotherapy put her in remission and today she is considered wholly cured. But there was a waiting period before that proclamation could be made, and during that waiting period there were regular trips to Buffalo for bone marrow exams. The little girl's father would take her to Buffalo and her mother would remain home. And every time, matters hung in the balance for these parents. What would the bone marrow declare: continuing health or a backward step? At the time these friends lived across the street from us, and we would do what we could for Pat during those days of suspended balance as she waited for the phone call from her husband. But Pat was a private person and as I recall it, we actually did very little for her. Pat knew we were there; she knew she could come over if she wanted to; she knew we would be glad to come to her home. Each time dad and daughter went to Buffalo, we would do something to let her know that we knew this particular day was her day of waiting.

Maybe David's court officials tried too hard. Maybe they wanted to provide too much structure for their beleagured king.

Miscalculation

When the child finally died, the court officials were frightened to tell David. They feared he might do something rash. "How can we tell him that his child is dead? He might do himself some harm!" (2 Samuel 12:18 TEV)

Have you ever underestimated the ability of another to cope? Sometimes we overestimate, but I have the sense that more often we underestimate. People who are seemingly frail or weak or needy or resourceless regularly surprise us when push comes to shove. They rise to occasions we — and perhaps they too — never thought possible.

Pentecost I

Harry Wiggins was an English teacher in my first congregation. He had married late in life and it was a happy marriage. But his wife became sick and eventually died. The day she died, Harry was out of town tending to some business and I was called. It fell to me to tell Harry of his wife's death, and it was not a task I relished. Harry was probably more dependant on his wife than she was on him, and I wondered how he would take the news of her death.

He came into the house and headed right for her bedroom. I gently headed him off, placed my hand on his shoulder, and told him of Mary's death. "Oh no," he groaned and then went into the room to be with her for a time.

Well, Harry surprised many of us. He took hold of what needed attention. He had never gotten a driver's license, and at seventy-some years of age went out and acquired one. He continued to write and publish poems. He commenced to write a regular historical column for his hometown newspaper. And he did a good bit of guest lay preaching in area churches. He led a full life until the day he joined his wife in death.

David surprised his court, too. No wool was being pulled over his eyes. He could sense that the child had died, and what he commenced to do stupefied them. He got up, took a bath, combed his hair, and changed his clothes. He then went and worshiped, and after that ate a full meal. He announced to his surprised court, "I did fast and weep while he was still alive. . . . But now that he is dead, why should I fast? I will some day go to where he is, but he can never come back to me." (2 Samuel 12:22-23 TEV)

I have a hunch that David was able to get on with his life because he had first entered wholeheartedly into that period when matters hung in the balance. He probably churned matters over and over again in his mind; he surely wrestled with his contributions to the darkness that was upon

Ordinary People, Extraordinary God

him. And out of all this there emerged some sense of resolution. What else could be done? Best to get on with life, regrettable as his sojourn with darkness had been.

Restoration

And that's what David did. God and David had worked matters out. They no longer hung in the balance and David moved on. "Then David comforted his wife Bathsheba. He had intercourse with her, and she bore a son, whom David named Solomon." (2 Samuel 12:24 TEV)

It is part of the wonder and glory of God that God doesn't leave his children suspended forever between failure and uncertainty. God, as that most beloved of Psalms reminds us, restores our souls and leads us into avenues of righteousness.

Runaway Lives

Proper 14   *2 Samuel 18:1, 5, 9-15*

For cowboy lovers, the 1950s were golden. There were more cowboys than you can count on your fingers and toes: Hopalong Cassidy, and Gene Autry, Roy Rogers, The Lone Ranger, Lash LaRue and the list goes on. There were probably only a dozen or so basic scenarios played out in all their shows, and one of the classics was the runaway stagecoach. The driver became incapacitated, the horses went mad, the coach was full of terrified passengers, and along came Roy riding Trigger at what seemed like seventy-five miles an hour. He pulled up next to the runaway horses, leaped onto the back of a lead horse, and brought the stagecoach to a safe stop. Remember all that?

This episode from the eighteenth chapter of 2 Samuel is about runaway lives. In fact, that's true for much of 1 and 2 Samuel. Certain forces have been set into play, are gaining momentum, and might very possibly become the keepers of the people who once kept them.

Ever notice how often in life the balance subtly shifts, and what we were intended to keep now keeps us?

The Prime Movers

Look at the prime movers in this drama, a drama that actually goes back several chapters.

Absalom: We first gain a flavor for this son of David in connection with the rape of his attractive sister Tamar. Her fate so enrages him that he eventually kills her abuser. The forces of rage become his keeper. Since Tamar's abuser is a step-brother to Absalom, this leads to tension in his relationship with his father, and there ensues a period of estrangement between the two. A bit later Absalom begins to entertain political aspirations and he moves to undermine his father's rule. These aspirations lead to Absalom eventually becoming literally hung-up in a tree by his hair. (I always knew there were some advantages to being bald.)

Joab: He was one of David's most loyal and effective military commanders. He is so loyal in fact, that he becomes caught by his zeal for a military victory in David's behalf and disobey's David's wish that his son Absalom not be harmed. Not only does Joab run afoul of David's wishes, he is downright truculent in his treatment of the suspended Absalom.

David: We have already seen in other stories that David, too, could find himself kept by runaway forces. That's precisely what the story of David and Bathsheba is all about.

Consequences

Clearly runaway-ness has consequences. It has a consuming quality inasmuch as it turns upon the person who is intended to be its keeper and so twists and distorts that person that his/her life becomes miserable and warped. It costs Absalom his life, Joab (it appears) his military position, and David grief on more than one occasion.

Pentecost I

In our day, for example, it cost Richard Nixon the Oval Office; Oliver North public censure and criminal prosecution; and as we have seen recently, the Exxon Corporation much money in controversial attempts to clean up Alaskan waters.

What's more, its scope is inclusive. When runaway-ness grips our lives and we are out of control, other lives are affected, too. Families where there is substance abuse know that all too well, as do families that must cope with a workaholic or a despot.

One of Aesop's fables is about a young mouse in search of adventure. As he is running along the bank of a pond, he is seen by a frog who swims to the bank and croaks: "Won't you pay me a visit? I can promise you a good time if you do."

The mouse doesn't need much coaxing, for it is a bright world out there, but there is a problem. The mouse can't swim and doesn't wish to venture very far out into the pond.

The frog has a plan. He ties the mouse's leg to his own with a tough reed. Then he jumps into the pond, dragging his foolish companion with him.

The mouse has soon had enough, but the deceiving frog has something else in mind. He pulls the mouse under the water and drowns him.

But before he can untie the reed that is binding him to the now dead mouse, a hawk comes sailing over the pond, swoops down, and seizes the mouse with the frog dangling from its leg. In one fell swoop, he has both meat and fish for dinner.

Runaway-ness has that quality about it. It swoops down and affects not just the one, but often the many.

A Modest Hero

But there is in this story a modest hero. I say modest because he is as realistic as he is idealistic. But I say hero because he gives evidence of resisting forces which are sweeping everyone else along.

Ordinary People, Extraordinary God

We don't even know this man's name, but he is one of David's men and he is the one who discovers Absalom hanging in the tree, and reports it to Joab. Joab responds, "If you saw him, why didn't you kill him on the spot? I myself would have given you ten pieces of silver and a belt." (2 Samuel 18:11 TEV) The report says that twenty-thousand men were killed; David's troops were on a roll. And, Joab reasons, why wouldn't this unnamed trooper put the frosting on the cake by immediately dispatching the man who caused it all in the first place? But the man wouldn't do it, and he gives his reason:

> *Even if you gave me a thousand pieces of silver, I wouldn't lift a finger against the king's son. We all heard the king command you and Abishai and Ittai, "For my sake don't harm the young man Absalom." But if I had disobeyed the king and killed Absalom, the king would have heard about it — he hears about everything — and you would not have defended me.*
>
> (2 Samuel 18:12-13 TEV)

This man's motives were mixed, but I still say we give him three cheers because he wouldn't allow himself to be kept by the forces that were keeping everyone else. He exercised his will and said no to them.

It was Carl Jung who offered this caveat years ago:

> *All mass movements, as one might expect, slip with the greatest ease down an inclined plane represented by large numbers. Where the many are, there is security; what the many believe must of course be true; what the many want must be worth striving for, and necessary, and therefore good. In the clamor of the many there lies the power to snatch wish-fulfillments by force; sweetest of all, however, is that gentle and painless slipping back into the kingdom of childhood, into the paradise of parental care, into happy-go-luckiness and irresponsibility. All the thinking and*

looking after are done from the top; to all questions there is an answer; and for all needs the necessary provision is made. The infantile dream state of the mass man is so unrealistic that he never thinks to ask who is paying for this paradise. The balancing of accounts is left to a higher political or social authority, which welcomes the task, for its power is thereby increased; and the more power it has, the weaker and more helpless the individual becomes.
(*The Undiscovered Self*, pp. 70-71)

That describes people not only politically and socially, but also religiously.

Jesus put it more succinctly: "Blessed are those who are persecuted for righteousness' sake, for theirs is the kingdom of heaven." (Matthew 5:10)

Remember the runaway stagecoach? All of our lives become, at some point or another, runaway lives, and we become caught up in forces that appear larger than life and seem to demand our blind obedience. This happens in our families, our places of vocation, and even in the church. But I like to think of God as coming alongside these runaway forces, leaping upon them, and bringing our runaway lives to a halt and returning them to us.

I can't tell you how this happens, because it happens to everybody differently. It happened to the Gerasene demoniac in the tombs; it happened to Saint Paul on the Damascus Road; it happened to the man ill at the pool side after a grip of thirty-eight years. But it has happened, is happening and will continue to happen.

And a good place to begin is to ask God to come alongside, leap onto these runaway forces in us, and bring them under control. Hosea's picture of God encourages us:

Ordinary People, Extraordinary God

> *I will heal their faithlessness;*
> *I will love them freely . . .*
> *They shall return and dwell beneath my shadow,*
> *they shall flourish as a garden;*
> *they shall blossom as the vine,*
> *their fragrance shall be like the*
> *wine of Lebanon.*
>
> (Hosea 14:4, 7)

Trust that. Can't you see God coming alongside — right now?

From Mourning to Morning

Proper 15 *2 Samuel 18:24-33*

It was a perfectly lovely day and we had no reason to suspect that it would be anything but a typically happy Saturday — a day to run errands, wash the cars and anticipate an evening with friends. But that all changed when, around 1:30 p.m., a phone call came from my wife's father in Cleveland indicating that her mother had unexpectedly died. A week earlier she had had a heart attack, but a full recuperation had been the prognosis, and so this word came as shock and radical disruption. Suddenly and without warning, we were all catapulted into the experience of grief. Within a few hours we were airborne, making our dazed way toward a rendevous with a major loss. Intellectually, of course, we had known that such a day was inevitable, but now that day in reality had arrived, and grief had set upon us.

Most of us have had similar experiences, and while none relish talking about death and grief, they need to be explored. What's more, our faith is not silent about them. In fact, our faith contends that grief holds great promise for us all. Far from being a spoilsport, grief, as our faith sees it, is deliverer and healer. Phillips translates Jesus' celebrated lines like this: "How happy are those who know what sorrow means, for they will be given courage and comfort!" (Matthew 5:5) If I understand those words at all correctly, they are positive, promise-bearing, and restorative words. They also underscore the appropriateness of David's reaction to the death of his son Absalom:

> *The king was overcome with grief. He went up to the room over the gateway and wept. As he went, he cried, "O my son! My son Absalom! Absalom, my son! If only I had died in your place, my son!"*
>
> (2 Samuel 18:33)

Not an Aberration

Because we tend to sweep discussions of grief under the rug, there is always the risk that someone will assume there is something abnormal or unusual about it. But nothing could be further from the truth. Grief is not aberrant; it is salutary. Ironically, it only becomes pathological when it has been mismanaged in the first place. So if life, for whatever reason, has summoned you to be sad, be glad for the sadness. Your grief is God's plan to help you feel better.

Actually, there are gradations of grief. It is not, alone, the feeling we have when someone we love dies. When mother or father takes a job in another town, there can be a sadness about that departure for everyone in the family. That's grief, too. There is grief when a pet dies, when a friend moves away, and when we say farewell to one stage of life so that we can embrace another. Robert Johnson reminds us that even weddings have an element of grief in them:

Pentecost I

> Many of our wedding customs are actually funeral customs. In primitive weddings, marriage was celebrated as such; it was at once a funeral, a transformation, and a joyous outburst.
>
> (*She*, p. 11)

Not a Time for Heroics

Keep in mind, too, that grief should never be construed as a summons to heroic behavior. I'm always a bit uneasy when, immediately following a death, I am told that those most directly affected are doing just fine. When a connection to one who has died has been one of profound and constructive bondedness, one does not "do well" when first it is terminated.

Following her husband's death at sixty-four years of age, Anne Brooks kept a journal for the first six months of widowhood. At the sixth-month point, she made this entry:

> *I still certainly am not fine. Nor whole, but I am functioning to the best of my limits. The limits define themselves at the strangest times and places. Shopping in a country store and wanting to share a "find" will bring tears to my eyes. "Mack the Knife" on the car radio, one of our favorite dance tunes, kept me crying for miles along a lonely stretch of road. The way my son ran along the station platform to greet me was so much like his father. These things hurt, and hurt painfully.*
>
> (*The Grieving Time*, p. 33)

At the end of her journal Anne Brooks adds, "This is a testament to love and loss. To withhold grief is destructive; to release it, healing. The writing of this book was my life-line. May the reading help your grieving time. You are not alone." (p. 35)

Ordinary People, Extraordinary God

A few years back, a colleague experienced his father's death and it was his desire to preside at his dad's funeral. My wife and I attended, and how we wished that our friend would have allowed himself to be a grieving son and not a strong pastor. His mother sat in the front pew with relatives; his wife sang in the choir; and he conducted the service. There were times when he came close to crying, but always regained his composure. I think the saddest time of the service for me, given the fact that I knew his father in only the slightest way, was at the end. My friend was preceding his father's casket out of the church building, and as I turned and looked again in the direction of the chancel, I saw his wife sobbing and being comforted by a young boy from the church youth group. I had the strongest feeling that there was a decided misalignment about the whole arrangement. Role confusion is what it was. It was not a time for pastoral heroics; it was a time for the expression of very human feelings of grief because of loss. It was a time for a son to mourn.

Resource That Bolster

In our grief we are helped beyond measure by other people. More than once, grieving people have told me how they were struck by the outpouring of care and support. People have a very spontaneous and wonderful way of surrounding us when we need them. They send notes, bring in food, offer to run errands, and sit with us.

Sometimes they will tell us that they don't know precisely what to say. That Saturday when my mother-in-law died, some friends took us to the airport. As he was putting our luggage into the trunk of his car, Ed remarked: "I just don't know what to say at a time like this." We responded, "You don't have to say anything. It's enough that you are here with us."

Pentecost I

There are no right words for occasions like that. I would even go so far as to say that it doesn't make a great deal of difference what words you choose. People in need will read our feelings, not analyze our choice of vocabulary.

Then, too, our Christian understanding helps heal us. For Christian people, death is neither a bogeyman nor a robber. It's influence is both limited and passing. Death is not a wall, but a door; not alone an ending, but also a beginning; not an enemy, but a friend; not a squelcher, but a liberator. Hence, "Death is swallowed up in victory. O death, where is thy victory? O death, where is thy sting." (1 Corinthians 15:55)

While it may be hard for us to articulate the nature of survival beyond the grave, it is enough to know that God cares and that Jesus Christ has gone before us. While some on this matter are so specific as to be arrogant, others are so silent as to be faithless. Thank God, then, for people like Samuel Miller, who steer a true course between arrogance and silence. Wrote Miller: "We may have a thousand doubts and be constrained by the most courageous candor, but we believe that death does not have the last word. Life has depths in it which death does not touch; it has heights which death cannot reach; it has powers which death cannot quell." (*Man the Believer*, pp. 139-140)

Following his mother's death in 1978, Henri Nouwen recorded his pilgrimage of grief in a volume he entitled *In Memoriam*. In that journal he writes of how his grief became a kind of seedbed for religious growth.

> *The deeper I entered into my own grief, the more I became aware that something new was about to be born, something I had not known before. . . . Mother's death is God's way of converting me, of letting his Spirit set me free. It is all still very new. A great deal has happened in these weeks, but what will happen in the months and years ahead*

> will be far more than I can understand. I am still waiting, yet already receiving; still hoping, yet already possessing; still wondering, yet already knowing. . . . Sometimes I find myself daydreaming about radical changes, new beginnings and great conversions. Yet I know that I must be patient and allow her who taught me so much by her life to teach me even more by her death.
>
> (pp. 59, 61-62)

It is the witness of many brothers and sisters in Christ that our mourning can be, at the hands of God and God's people, transformed into a new and bright morning. I leave you with the witness of Frances Gray:

> *The first year was gone on December 19, and now I know why everyone says it's so bad. All your memories that year are "we" memories. Then suddenly you remember something which happened, and you can say, "I did so-and-so a year ago. . . ."*
>
> *My life is beginning to be different, slightly but detectably, almost like a changing wind. . . .*
>
> *"O sing unto the Lord a new song; for He hath done marvelous things."*

Swansong as Themesong

Proper 16 *2 Samuel 23:1-7*

Have you ever fantasized about what you might say, if given the opportunity, on the last day of your working career to your friends and colleagues who had gathered to hear you? The room is full, a hush has fallen over the group, and your moment has come. What might you say to your fellow teachers, or factory workers, or business associates? I'm not thinking so much of the retirement party, because they tend to be lighter affairs. Rather, I am thinking about your last full and authentic day on the job. In my own case I have sometimes asked myself, What will I preach about the last time I am in the pulpit? What will be the content of my homiletical swansong?

Even as I paint this picture I am aware of some who will say in response, "I sure hope they give me the opportunity to take a few parting shots; I'll be glad to give them an earful!" I know ministers who would so speak and you know people in your field of endeavor who would be similarly inclined.

Authentic Swansong

But authentic swansongs are not of that ilk. David's last words make that clear.

His words are affirmative without being arrogantly dogmatic: "The spirit of the Lord speaks through me; his message is on my lips." (2 Samuel 23:2 TEV) My translation: Our lives, if they don't stand for something, are less than they are intended to be. Often, tragically less.

When I was growing up, I played the trumpet. In fact I owned two of them. I had a sentimental attachment to them, but some years ago I sold one to an antique dealer. It really didn't make any sense to keep it; I had not seriously played it since 1965. Since that time, no air had been blown into its mouthpiece, and no music had come forth from its bell.

Human lives can often be thought of in those terms. Nothing is being blown into them and nothing is emerging from them. They are just there. Day follows day with breakfast, lunch, dinner and bed, but nothing is happening. No winds from God are being granted entrance into them and resultantly, no fruit is being produced. Money, maybe even big money, is being made, but it is quickly understood that minus some sense of linkage to what ultimately matters, nothing matters. That sense of futility and emptiness, so known to people like Camus and Kafka, begins to do its insidiously undermining work.

The psalmist's words are also hopeful without being delusive:

> *The God of Israel has spoken; the protector of Israel said to me: "The king who rules with justice, who rules in reverence for God, is like the sun shining on a cloudless dawn, the sun that makes the grass sparkle after rain." And that is how God will bless my descendants, because he has made an eternal covenant with me, an agreement that will not be broken, a promise that will not be changed.*
> (2 Samuel 23:3-5 TEV)

Pentecost I

My translation: Behave in accordance with God's wishes and hope will be as "sun shining on a cloudless dawn . . ."

The biblical drama from beginning to end is about God's covenant with his people, a covenant of steadfast love, and for that reason, we continue to announce, as Jeremiah announced to the people of his day, "There is hope for your future." (Jeremiah 31:17 TEV)

Remember those dark days in your life — those days you would just as soon forget? We like to forget them because the darkness was so dark. But remembering them, we remember too just how precious a commodity hope then was. Maybe the vessel of hope was a friend, or a passage of Scripture, or a religious experience, or a line from a book. The point is, it kept us going; it dissuaded us from giving up; it made suicide a less attractive option.

Victor Frankl, in his celebrated book *Man's Search For Meaning*, tells of a fellow concentration camp prisoner who related one of his dreams. In the dream this man was told that he could have answered any question he wished. He reported to Frankl: "I wanted to know when we, when our camp, would be liberated and our sufferings come to an end." (p. 119) The prisoner had the dream in February, 1945. Frankl asked him when the dream told him his sufferings would come to an end, and he furtively and in a whisper answered that it was to be March 30th.

When he reported this dream to Frankl he was full of hope and convinced that his dream would be fulfilled. As that date approached, it became unlikely that the camp would be liberated by then. On March 29th, the man suddenly became ill and ran a high temperature. On March 30th, the day of liberation according to his dream, this man became delirious and lost consciousness. And on March 31st of that year, he was dead. Frankl writes that to all outward appearances, typhus was the cause of the man's death. But it was the absence of hope that had caused this man's demise.

Ordinary People, Extraordinary God

Faith's swansongs instill hope in people's hearts. Gene Bartlett, in his swansong titled *Postscript to Preaching*, writes of his generation's attitude as they enter the postlude time of their ministries:

> *Many of the things we thought would happen did not happen, and many we thought couldn't happen, have happened. Yet today I want to bear witness that many in my generation are not in despair. To the contrary, we have come into a kind of heady hope which no longer rests upon the evidences that a secular day can bring forth. What is that hope? It rests where the biblical hope must rest, namely, in the nature and word of God as it has been disclosed to us.*
> (p. 78)

Then David's words are realistic without being disparaging: "But godless men are like thorns that are thrown away; no one can touch them barehanded." (2 Samuel 23:6 TEV) My translation: Behavior has consequences. Ever think that people in our day believe just the opposite — that they believe you can behave as you want to and it won't make any difference? Eat anything you want to, give yourself away indiscriminately, say anything you want to, violate body, mind and soul, raise the children any way you desire — it's all immaterial.

Yet again and again, evidence appears to the contrary. It all does make a difference. Let small children wander from pillar to post and fend for themselves as best they can, and they will be damaged. Eat too much, and your body will rise up in protest. Exercise no control over what you say and when you say it, and you will not experience fulfilling relationships. Exercise no limits over how and on whom you spend yourself, and there will be an inner-erosion of integrity that does cause pain.

Pentecost I

Swansongs set alternatives before us. They tell us of our options, as Moses in his swansong related them to the people of his day: "... this day ... I have set before you life and death ... therefore choose life ..." (Deuteronomy 30:19)

A Gathering Point

In a day of what can easily become a confusing pluralism, it is well for us to have access to moments when we can hear again what is central for Christian people, and swansongs of faith can do that for us. They can become gathering points where we can once more get our bearings of faith. These gathering points of affirmation, hopefulness and decision inspire and direct us.

Years back, I learned of a young minister named Glen Brown who had died very early in his ministry. He saw his death coming and kept a journal during those months of decline. At one point he made this entry:

> *Where do you get the courage to respond to those basic conditions of human existence which are your teachers? Is it self-derived? Surely when we are in the midst of it, overcome by frustration and disappointment or doubt or fear we don't believe that any courage that we have is self-derived. ... Is courage derived from others? But then, if it is, who helps those who are helpers when they are in need? Or is courage from beyond you? ... You have to answer that question. ... For me courage is from beyond. Beyond my own strength, yet working within my own strength and this is the paradox of it. From God who is the source and sustainer of my very existence as a human being.*
> (From a sermon preached by Gene Bartlett at Colgate Rochester Divinity School, "More Than Conquerors," November 18, 1965.)

Ordinary People, Extraordinary God

The bottom line of it all? Swansongs make good themesongs. It is well for us to soak our minds and souls and hearts in the wisdom of those who have approached the top of the mountain of truth. They give us the supplies we need for our journeys, the staples we need to continue. They give us themesongs that can be sung in our hearts. Then one day, when we rise to give our swansong, we can do for someone else what others long ago did for us. In that way, our faith is transmitted and the good news of God's salvation is made available to those who will follow us.

www.ingramcontent.com/pod-product-compliance
Lightning Source LLC
Chambersburg PA
CBHW060846050426
42453CB00008B/849